FABRIC
HARMONY

A DECORATING GUIDE TO CREATIVE FABRIC AND COLOR COMBINATIONS FOR THE HOME

ROCKPORT
PUBLISHERS

Tara McLellan

First published in the United States of America by

Rockport Publishers, Inc.

33 Commercial Street

Gloucester, Massachusetts 01930-5089

Telephone: (978) 282-9590

Fax: (978) 283-2742

www.rockpub.com

ISBN 1-56496-856-1

10 9 8 7 6 5 4 3 2 1

Design: Judy Arisman

Layout and Production: Susan Raymond

Cover Image: Bobbie Bush Photography

Back cover photo credits:

©Laura Ashley Limited 2001, left; Donghia Furniture & Textiles, all others

Project Manager: Judy Schurger

Special thanks to Laura Ashley Limited

Printed in China

CONTENTS

INTRODUCTION

Whether it's viscose or velvet, broadcloth or brocade, choosing the right fabrics for a home can be overwhelming. From hemp to silk to manufactured fibers, the quality, texture, and patterns available today are astounding. *Fabric Harmony* is intended as a road map to guide you through the countless options; help you identify fabrics and their appropriate uses; and inspire you in utilizing fabrics throughout your home to create a mood that is right for you.

Each fabric has its own look and feel, a certain weight in the hand. Fabrics can stand alone or in combination to add a unique life, texture, motion, and emotion to a room. They can transform a monochromatic look from flat to flirtatious, make a modern, bold statement, or create a restful retreat from the outside world.

Home decorating with fabric is easy and rewarding. Simple accents such as pillow coverings, draperies, slipcovers, and tablecloths provide quick ways to add color to or change the mood of a room. More dramatic presentations such as floor-to-ceiling chintz, a treasured tapestry wall hanging, or an exotic canopied bed can create other worlds within a room. Fabrics can be modern, exotic, and on the cutting edge of design trends, or classic, refined, and enduring. They can be feminine or masculine or a combination of the two. Color palettes can range from cool, with overall neutrals, crisp whites, and watery pastels, to hot, featuring spicy flavors, robust earth hues, or rich jewel tones. In other words, designing with fabric is only as limited as your own imagination.

Fabric Harmony provides all of the essential information on fabric types and content; demonstrates new ideas for designing with fabric—choosing colors, combining patterns, and introducing texture—for the look you want; and inspires the designer within to transform every room of the home with fabric. It is a compass that points the way to discovering styles to suit any space, any personality, and any lifestyle and guides you in creating the mood that you envision. Get inspired, get creative, and get started.

ABOVE: A stack of pretty fabrics is like an artist's palette. The possibilities of creation are endless.

OPPOSITE: Keeping a scrapbook of your favorite fabrics and color combinations helps when putting together a look that that feels right for you and your home.

HOW TO USE THIS BOOK

Fabric Harmony categorizes fabrics into twelve easy-to-identify moodways to simplify the design and decorating process. Do not let these divisions constrain your decorating, however. Moods may be shuffled, mixed, and matched for a totally unique look to suit your home and personal style. Each of the twelve chapters contains thirty-six fabric swatches as a starting point for guidance and inspiration. Fabric name, colorway, content, and manufacturer are given as a reference, as well as suggested color accents to work with. Great fabrics can be found anywhere, from a salvage bin at a local notions shop to a couture fabric boutique. Check for vintage treasures from your grandmother's sewing chest stashed in the attic or at a secondhand shop. Look to fabrics already on hand to be recycled into one-of-a-kind pieces. Simple fabrics, such as a classically clean cotton calico, can be just as beautiful as the most expensive silk brocade if applied to the correct room and in the appropriate manner. This book offers examples of where and when to use each fabric quality and style, from ticking to tapestry, and gets you started on the road to decorating with fabric.

 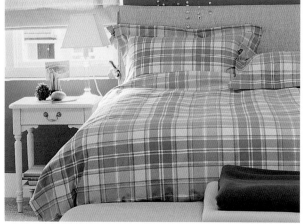

"Buzz Off" *by Donghia*
Linen
Cotton 100%

INSIDE FABRIC   A Who's Who and What's What on Fabric

NATURAL FABRICS

Fabric	Composition	Characteristics	Good Uses	Special Considerations
Camel	camel, alpaca, llama hair	lustrous, strong, good insulator	blankets, throws, classic look	expensive, resists dyes
Cashmere	the fleece of Kashmir goats	ultimate in luxury, softness	blankets, throws	expensive, must be dry cleaned
Cotton	fibers from the cotton plant	comfortable, soft, versatile and inexpensive, dyes/prints easily, washable, can be used almost anywhere in the home, easy to sew	upholstery, curtains, bed/bath linens, table linens	
Hemp	fibers from the hemp plant	three times stronger than cotton, durable, breathable, softens without weakening, washable	curtains, table linens, towels	not as soft as other fibers, wrinkles easily
Linen	fibers from the flax plant	soft, twice as strong as cotton, crisp, dyes/prints easily	upholstery, curtains, bed/bath linens, table linens	wrinkles easily, must be hand washed or dry cleaned
Mohair	angora goat hair	strong, luxurious, soft, good insulator, dyes well	upholstery, rugs, blankets	most resilient non-crushable quality, best fabric for high-traffic areas
Silk	fibers from silk worm	soft, crisp, luxurious, dyes/prints well, drapes well	curtains, upholstery, table linens, bed linens	poor resistance to fading, must be hand washed or dry cleaned
Wool	fibers from sheep fleece	washable, dyes easily, comfortable, durable, soft, luxurious, good insulator	a practical choices for most areas of the home, carpets, drapes, upholstery, blankets, bed linens	wrinkle resistant makes it versatile

Source: Fabric University, www.fabriclink.com

MANUFACTURED FABRICS

FABRIC	COMPOSITION	CHARACTERISTICS	GOOD USES	SPECIAL CONSIDERATIONS
ACETATE	from wood pulp or cotton linters	luxurious, crisp, soft, dyes/prints easily, durable, resilient	drapes, upholstery	must be dry cleaned
ACRYLIC	man-made fibers	lightweight, soft, warm, dyes easily, easy to care for and has wool-like appearance, washable, resilient, durable	blankets, rugs, upholstery	
NYLON	man-made fibers	lightweight, strong, washable, resilient, durable	rugs, drapes, upholstery	poor resistance to long exposure to sunlight
POLYESTER	man-made fibers	strong, crisp, soft, resilient, washable, wrinkle resistant	drapes, rugs, upholstery	can be blended with dry-clean-only fabrics to give them extra life and washability
RAYON	from wood pulp	soft, dyes/prints easily, drapes well	bedding, drapes, table linens, upholstery	some rayons are washable and some are not, so read the care label carefully

FABRIC TYPES

FABRIC	COMPOSITION	CHARACTERISTICS	GOOD USES	SPECIAL CONSIDERATIONS
BROCADE	cotton, linen, silk	heavy, raised all-over pattern or floral design	upholstery, drapes	heavy fabric requires extra support on window coverings
CALICO	cotton, linen	tightly woven, all-over print	drapes, bed linens, table linens	bright, sunny prints create classic and country looks for breakfast rooms, kitchens, and bedrooms
CHAMBRAY	cotton, linen, silk, crisp cotton chambray	plain woven manufactured material	pillows, bed linens	usually makes for comfortable and washable bed linens
CHIFFON	silk, rayon	sheer, airy, soft	sheers, bed curtains	the silkiest and softest of sheers creates fresh, airy, and romantic effects for floor-to-ceiling window coverings or bed curtains
CHINTZ	cotton, silk	a weave of fabric that has been glazed for a clean, polished look	upholstery, drapes, slipcovers	the shine of a richly patterned chintz adds elegant color and depth to dining, living, or bedrooms

Fabric Types—continued

Fabric	Composition	Characteristics	Good Uses	Special Considerations
Damask	linen, cotton, silk	flat, all-over patterns in complementary colors, reversible	wallcovering, upholstery, drapery, table linens	the subtle pattern of a complementary colored damask is a good way to add pattern to a refined dining, living, or bedroom
Gingham	cotton	woven fabric with an all-over plaid or check pattern	pillows, table linens, medium-weight curtains	brightly colored gingham patterns give a clean, lively look to bedrooms, sunny breakfast rooms, and kitchens
Houndstooth Check	cotton, wools, linen	a twill-weave fabric with a broken check pattern	upholstery, pillows	this classic pattern will pass muster for years, creates a more masculine look in libraries and living rooms
Madras	cotton	a lightweight pastel shaded, breathable checked, plaid, or striped cotton woven fabric	curtains, bed/bath linens	madras creates a fresh seaside look for bed or bath
Tapestry	linen, silk, cotton	a heavy, often handwoven fabric	wall hangings, upholstery	heavy, expensive and precious, tapestries featuring a historical or pictorial display provide a luxurious and elegant touch as wall hangings, on pillows, or on grand upholstered pieces
Ticking	linen, cotton	tightly woven, durable material, originally used to cover mattresses, pillows, and work clothes	bed/bath linens, pillows, upholstery, curtains	this durable material, with its subtle, crisp, striped pattern creates a classic or country look for any room in the home
Velvet	silk, linen, cotton	luxurious piled material	upholstery, pillows	luxurious and silky soft, velvets are best in low-traffic areas due to their easily crushable nature

TIMELESS CLASSICS

Function and form

Pinstriped cottons. Soft flannels. Crisp linens. Classic fabrics all embody the same beautiful and functional qualities: simplicity, understated elegance, and versatility.

These simple, forgiving fabrics and patterns are not limited by time or space. Choose neutral-toned beige, white, or cream as a base for understated elegance. Add warmer shades, such as maroons and browns, or cooler ones, such as navy blue and hunter green, to add depth of feeling. Then, introduce pattern—sedate plaids, pretty pinstripes, and playful houndstooth checks— in bright colors, from antique gold to ice blue to entertain the eye and to complement more conservative colors. Round out the mix with texture. A relaxed herringbone, velvety corduroy, or understated wool flannel lends a softness that will keep a classic room infinitely touchable.

The lasting quality and ageless beauty of classic fabrics move effortlessly from room to room and from year to year.

Think the Parthenon or Shaker furniture. Classics create harmony and a peaceful, balanced, meditative mood. Neutral tones such as khaki, navy blue, and cream; the crisp lines of a gray pinstripe; or the clean pattern of a refined plaid transforms a room into the epitome of order and calm. Soft, clean textures such as brushed cotton or washed linen create a comfortable retreat without being overly fussy. Classics speak for themselves; they need no elaborate trim or complicated tailoring.

A traditional fabric or pattern highlights a beautiful piece of furniture without masking its lines or showcases a contrasting vibrant color or pattern. Classics work on their own, contrast and combine with other decorating schemes, and fit into any lifestyle and living space: a single's apartment, a newlyweds' love nest, a multigenerational family home, or a retiree condo.

ABOVE: Warm neutrals add subtle yet comfortable accents.

OPPOSITE: Soften a classic printed plaid curtain by pairing it with a simple floral print in complementary neutral shades.

Decorating with Classic Fabrics

Try using classic fabrics as the starting point of any decorating scheme. Use them on their own or with other styles for a balanced look. With fabrics as easy to work with and as versatile as these, decorating becomes uncomplicated and enjoyable. And when the fads fade, you'll still have elegant and timeless linen chairs, a crisply tailored sofa, or a treasured tablecloth.

For a timeless room, use a handsome piece of furniture as a focal point, such as a sofa with classic lines upholstered in soft, brushed, navy blue cotton. Add accents in golds, maroons, or dark greens for a more dressed-up look or pair with neutrals, natural linen, or chocolate brown, for example, for a more sedate look. Build on color with many layers of texture, from chenille to corduroy to felt, on accent pillows and furnishings, all cozy and inviting for an accessible, touchable feel. Finish the look with conservative, but definitely not sedate, trimmings to keep a room from becoming harsh. A contrasting cord trim, tiny vintage buttons, or a crisp box pleat or ruffles on pillows and window coverings invite a bit of lightness into the setting.

BUILD THE LOOK

CLASSIC COLOR COMBINATIONS REACH ACROSS THE COLOR WHEEL AS WELL AS AROUND IT. FOR SUBTLETY, TRY COMBINATIONS WITHIN THE SAME COLOR RANGE. MUTED TONES SHOULD GO WITH MUTED TONES, SUCH AS HEATHER BROWNS, BLUES, AND GRAYS. LIKEWISE, CRISP TONES WITH CRISP TONES CAN MAKE A CLASSIC PATTERN POP: THINK A WEDGWOOD BLUE-AND-GOLD PINSTRIPE OR A STRAIGHTFORWARD BLACK-AND-WHITE CHECKERBOARD.

OPPOSITE: A pair of blue china urns provides the color inspiration for this classically clean living room. Shades of the blue are repeated in plaids, solids, and florals on each upholstered piece. Golden highlights add contrast and shine.

Tips for Decorating
with Classic Fabrics

✦ Using fabrics as versatile as classics takes the guess-work out of decorating. For creating a contemporary classic look or for building on or tempering other mood-ways, try these techniques. Pair clean, classic fabrics—a natural linen or cotton, for instance—in subtle stripes and plaids to tone down a romantic look, soften a natural look, or relax a refined look. A crisply and simply tailored white linen pillow covering can easily move from a romantic bedroom to a fresh, airy sitting room to a refined, formal parlor room.

✦ Frame a picture-perfect view with a boxed valance of cream and navy blue. The neutral colors elegantly but unobtrusively enhance any scene.

✦ Opposites do attract. Boost the sex appeal of a shapely chair. The simple woven texture of unfussy linen can play straight man to the curves of an outrageous chair. Neutral toned accents can tame a wildly painted room. Try khaki and brown pillows along with a cream-colored upholstered sofa next to a cobalt-colored wall for a classically cool decor.

✦ For a more feminine look, stick to lighter weight whites and neutral naturals in pretty plaid and striped patterns. Pops of sage green and smoke blue add subtle color. For a more masculine look, use gray and brown suiting fabrics, pinstripes, and houndstooth checks in unexpected places: covering a comfy club chair or a tufted ottoman, or stretched across a padded headboard.

✦ Switch up accent pillows, drapes, and throws when the temperatures start to change. For fall and winter, try heather gray, navy blue, and maroon felts and wools. Spring and summer need clean white on whites, naturals, and nature-inspired shades of moss green and soft blue on breathable linens and cottons.

ABOVE: Recycle men's suiting fabrics for a classic look in unexpected places—a library ottoman or bedroom throw pillows. Pair with feminine floral brocades to round out the look.

OPPOSITE: Simple blue-and-white checks provide a lively contrast to a clean, neutral linen-covered headboard and bench for a refreshingly modern take on a classic look. Select tones from the pattern for wall paint, floor coverings, and accent blankets to maintain consistency.

Classic color palette

Like classic fabrics, classic colors combinations are charming and confident, cozy yet formal. Comfortable, favorite colors with shades and tints of blue take a leading role. Familiar and easy, classic colors will help create lasting interior style.

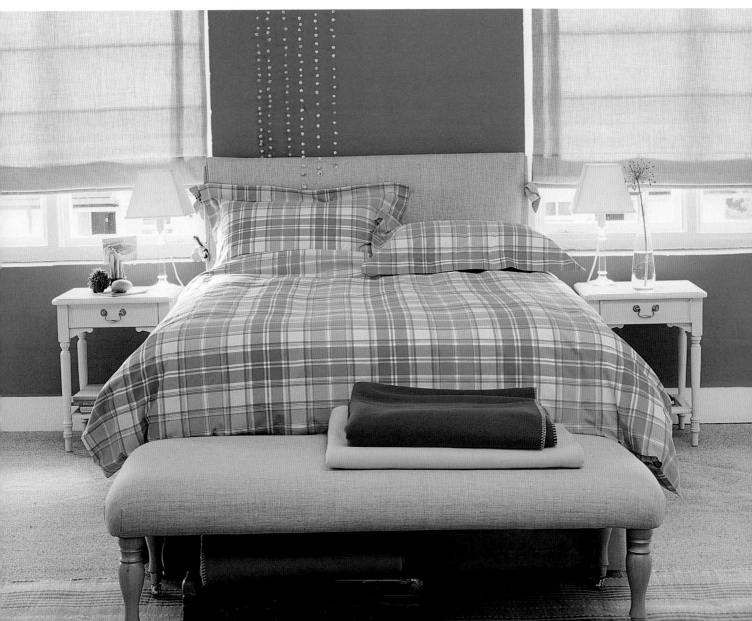

Classic Fabric Combinations

"Sleigh" *by Gretchen Bellinger*
Churned Butter
Wool 100%

"Scheherezade" *by Gretchen Bellinger*
Raven
Silk 100%

"Prospect House" *by Gretchen Bellinger*
Charcoal
Cotton 100%

"Awning" *by Gretchen Bellinger*
White/Beige
Cotton 100%

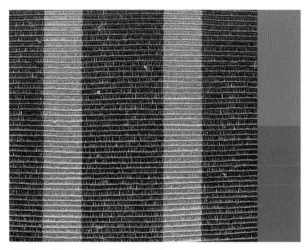

"Riviere Bievre" *by Classic Cloth*
Rosemary
Linen 67%, Viscose 33%

"Jamaica Stripe" *by Scalamandré*
Moss/Natural
Linen 67%, Viscose 33%

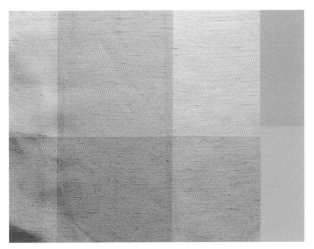

"Dorset Plaid" *by Scalamandré*
Taupe/Ecru/Grey
Linen 70%, Silk 30%

"Grand Otto" *by Classic Cloth*
Borage
Cotton 70%, Rayon 30%

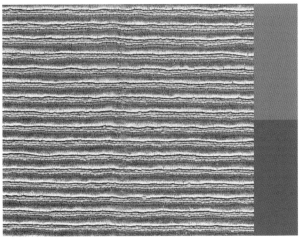

"Madeleine Silk Repp" *by Decorators Walk*
Ivory
Silk 100%

"Iron Stripe" *by Jim Thompson*
Delphi Blue
Silk 100%

"Foxtrot" *by Gretchen Bellinger*
Cream
Cotton 100%

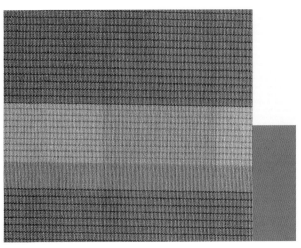

"Armande" *by Liberty Furnishings—Osborne & Little*
Moss/Natural
Viscose 60%, Cotton 40%

Classic Fabric Combinations

"Runabout" *by Gretchen Bellinger*
White
Cotton 100%

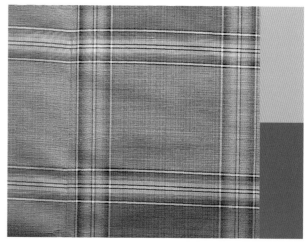

"Sumpter" *by Jim Thompson*
Wedgwood
Silk 100%

"Chesire" *by Lee Jofa*
Meringue
Rayon 73%, Nylon 27%

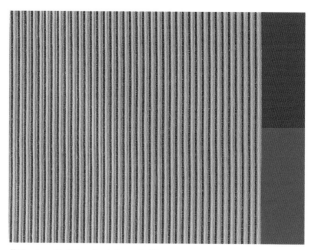

"Cinderella" *by Gretchen Bellinger*
Honey Butter
Cotton 68%, Viscose 32%

"Camel" *by Gretchen Bellinger*
Natural Camel
Camel Hair 100%

"Millbrook Stripe" *by Cowtan & Towt*
Ivory
Silk 40%, Wool 39%, Linen 21%

"Skiana" *by Osborne & Little*
Blue
Cotton 60%, Viscose 40%

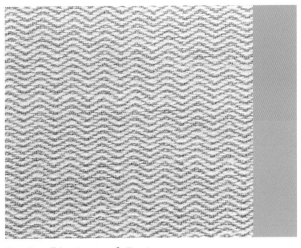

"Hudson" *by Cowtan & Towt*
Muslin
Cotton 52%, Linen 33%, Viscose 15%

"Canyon Tweed" *by Sina Pearson Textiles*
Bryce
Recycled Polyester 100%

"Comfort" *by Pollack & Associates*
Sky
Viscose 70%, Cotton 30%

"Cuddle Cloth" *by Knoll Textiles*
Haystack
Rayon 42%, Cotton 30%, Merino Wool 18%, Nylon 10%

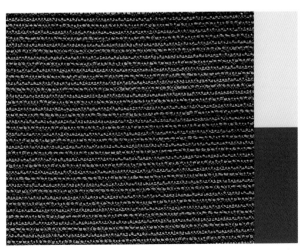

"River" *by Sina Pearson Textiles*
Clearwater
Recycled Polyester 100%

CLASSIC FABRIC COMBINATIONS

"Mercer" *by Jim Thompson*
Summer Night
Cotton 100%

"C210" *by Maharam*
C210/10
Saran 82%, Polyester 18%

"Arno" *by Knoll Textiles*
Flint
Wool 93%, Nylon 7%

"Halifax" *by Jim Thompson*
Camel
Silk 100%

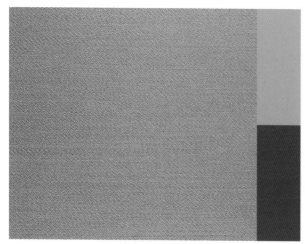

"Club Car" *by Pollack & Associates*
Dill
Wool 100%

"C220" *by Maharam*
C220/1
Saran 81%, Polyester 19%

"Cashmere" *by Gretchen Bellinger*
Black
Cashmere 100%

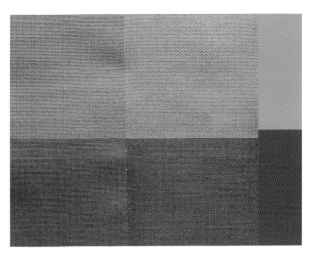

"Butterworth" *by Jim Thompson*
Highland Grey
Silk 100%

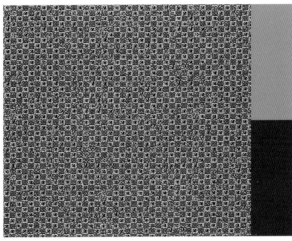

"Fractals Weave" *by Groundworks—Lee Jofa*
Fern
Viscose 51%, Polyester 49%

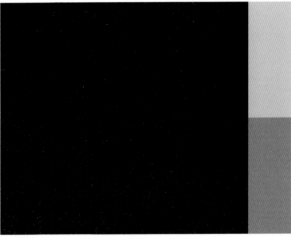

"Limousine Cloth" *by Gretchen Bellinger*
Porsche Prussian
Wool 100%

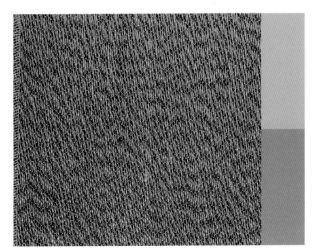

"Equine" *by Classic Cloth*
Pinto
Cotton 36%, Linen 25%, Rayon 39%

"Kilkenny" *by Classic Cloth*
Barley
Linen 74%, Wool 26%

MEMORABLE VINTAGE

Nostalgic and stylish

Vintage fabrics evoke feelings and memories of better times for a nostalgic look back. In an older home, they reflect their well-used, well-loved surroundings. In a contemporary or new home, they can lend a comfortable, warm tone.

Vintage means the very best that a particular era has to offer. From a design perspective, it means style that lasts a lifetime—and beyond. Search garage sales or your grandmother's attic for the best in vintage. Or look to the many fabric companies that provide new fabrics in vintage designs, fresh alternatives to perhaps more costly and well-worn material. New fabrics with old designs bring a warm look back but provide extra durability when used for upholstery or on a large area such as a window.

From antique embroideries to delicate lace and crewelwork to colorful and whimsical oilcloths, these fabrics have a life beyond their time.

Whether covering a sofa with soft, comfortable fabrics, immortalizing a treasured piece of embroidered work as art, or covering a kitchen work table with resilient, vintage oilcloth in nostalgic patterns, the home can indeed become a reflection of the heart and better times. Vintage fabrics make us feel good. They make us feel at home.

OPPOSITE: A soft stack of vintage textiles from Sarah Truitt, textile archivist, shows the subtle, well-worn shades of cherished linens from another time.

Sarah T

Decorating with Vintage Fabrics

From age-old linens to time-tested embroideries to newly made vintage designs, vintage fabrics span the ages for versatile and meaningful design. Preserve family-made heirlooms. A piece of family history, say a delicate lacework by a favorite aunt, comes alive again and is passed on to the next generation as a unique piece of framed art. Modernize a piece of your childhood. Turn the lively tangerine and avocado slipcovers your mom used into pop art pillows for a true homecoming every day.

Newly made fabrics with vintage designs bring a touch of whimsy into a room. Cheerful oilcloth designs from the 1930s are making a comeback on vinyl fabrics and their versatility is in evidence from tablecloths, placemats, and kitchen curtains to outdoor cushion and table coverings.

Vintage. Balance a bit of the old with the new. Hold on to a bit of history.

BUILD THE LOOK

USE BOLD, BRIGHT COLORS AND DESIGN, SUCH AS THE TRADITIONAL RED-AND-WHITE CHECKERED PICNIC PATTERN, ON TABLETOPS IN A SPARSELY DECORATED KITCHEN. STICK WITH MUTED COLORS FOR FLOOR COVERINGS SO AS NOT TO COMPETE WITH HARDWOOD OR PATTERNED FLOORING.

OPPOSITE: Choose fabrics with a faded look in pale pink, dusty rose, and antique white for a vintage look in new fabrics. Rich embroidered details in earthy greens, ochre, and rusts add a handmade quality.

Tips for Decorating
with Vintage Fabrics

✦ Use vintage fabrics along with new neutrals for a clean look with a past. Try a colorful embroidered piece with a new, tea-stained linen backing for a one-of-a-kind antique pillow at half the cost. Reclaim old curtain panels, upholstery, or tablecloths and give them new life as pillow covers or cleanly framed, distinctive artwork.

✦ A durable, bright oilcloth can be used as a convenient, easy-to-clean table-topper in an eat-in kitchen or transported to the picnic table for a cheerful barbecue with friends and family. Extremely hardworking, these nostalgic fabrics can also do double duty as economical area rugs in small spaces, as easy-to-clean curtains in a highly trafficked kitchen, or as placemats for a cheerfully set table.

✦ Clip swatches of favorite clothing before tossing them out for use in a memorable crazy quilt or in patchwork pillow for a country look with a snapshot of the past. Save interesting lace trim for unique details on tabletop linens. Use pretty scraps of material for unique drawer liners to protect sweaters and silks.

✦ Mismatched antique linens are always available at garage sales and secondhand shops. They are perfect for a crisply set table or for old fashioned hand towels in a guest bath. Conversely, try using antique table linens in the bedroom for delicate, feminine pillows and lacy bedside table covers for a cozy boudoir.

OPPOSITE: Hand-embroidered trims, such as these, are not only elegant and pleasing to the eye, but are also a part of history that can be passed down from generation to generation. Framing more fragile and meaningful pieces preserves them in a manner in which they can still be appreciated and enjoyed.

Vintage color palette

Vintage colors are an eclectic group ranging from saturated reds and yellows to shades of brown and green. The essence of these colors is in the nostalgic mood they create. Combined with vintage fabrics, they can bring to life times goneby.

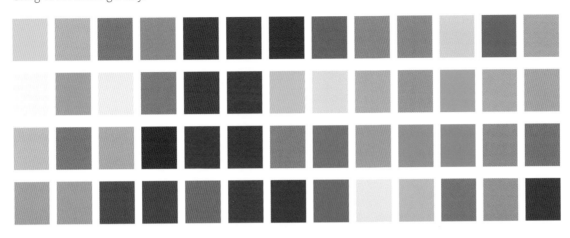

Vintage Fabric Combinations

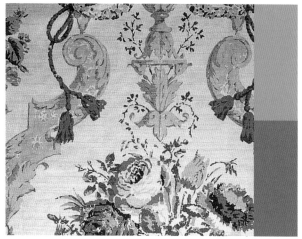

"Grosvenor House" *by Decorators Walk*
Rose/Yellow
Linen 59%, Cotton 41%

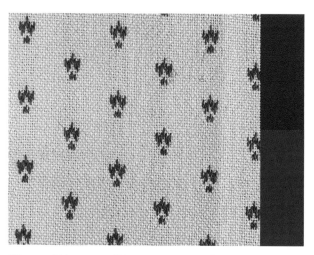

"Concord Homespun" *by Decorators Walk*
Cranberry/Natural
Linen 53%, Viscose 47%

"Somerfield Court" *by Decorators Walk*
Red/Hunter/Gold
Linen 59%, Cotton 41%

"Melton" *by Decorators Walk*
Multi/Ivory
Linen 59%, Cotton 41%

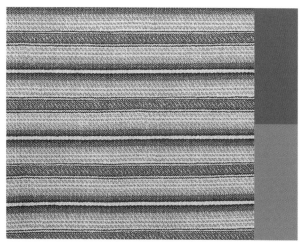

"Cortland Stripe" *by Decorators Walk*
Red
Linen 100%

"Wanstead Manor Print" *by Decorators Walk*
Multi
Linen 100%

"Devonshire House" *by Decorators Walk*
Rose/Yellow/Natural
Linen 59%, Cotton 41%

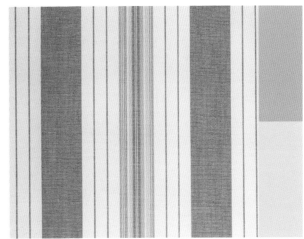

"Block Island" *by Decorators Walk*
Rose
Cotton 100%

"Grape Trellis" *by Decorators Walk*
Sterling
Linen 100%

"Folette" *by Rose Tarlow—Melrose House*
Taupe/Natural
Hemp Linen 100%

"Wild Irises Print" *by Mulberry at Lee Jofa*
Faded Green
Linen 52%, Cotton 36%, Nylon 12%

"Fiori" *by Rose Tarlow—Melrose House*
Doeskin/Natural
Hemp Linen 100%

Vintage Fabric Combinations

"Creed Lane" *by Decorators Walk*
Fern/Fawn
Linen 59%, Cotton 41%

"Edwin's Covey" *by Scalamandré*
Multi/Sisal
Linen 70%, Cotton 30%

"Vicenza" *by Rose Tarlow—Melrose House*
Amber/Wheat
Hemp Linen 100%

"Calais" *by Rose Tarlow—Melrose House*
Taupe/Natural
Hemp Linen 100%

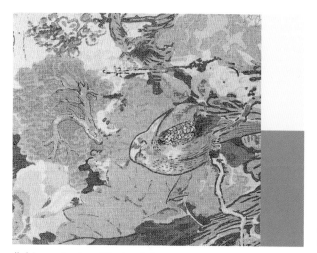

"Chinese Lantern" *by Lee Jofa*
Green/Yellow
Linen 100%

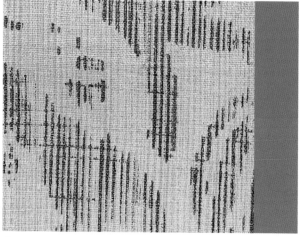

"Fleurette" *by Rose Tarlow—Melrose House*
Charcoal/Wheat
Hemp Linen 100%

"Roses in Squares" *by Oilcloth International*
Blue
Printed Vinyl

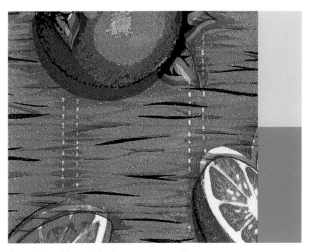

"Bamboo" *by Oilcloth International*
Blue
Printed Vinyl

"Pears and Apples" *by Oilcloth International*
Red/Yellow
Printed Vinyl

"Doily with Fruit" *by Oilcloth International*
Blue/Red
Printed Vinyl

"All Berries" *by Oilcloth International*
Red
Printed Vinyl

"Pears and Apples" *by Oilcloth International*
Yellow
Printed Vinyl

Vintage Fabric Combinations

"Bouquet" *by Oilcloth International*
Multi
Printed Vinyl

"Doily with Fruit" *by Oilcloth International*
Yellow
Printed Vinyl

"Big Apple" *by Oilcloth International*
Red/Yellow
Printed Vinyl

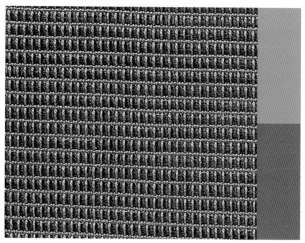

"Jewels" *by Classic Cloth*
Ruby
Cotton 58%, Viscose 42%

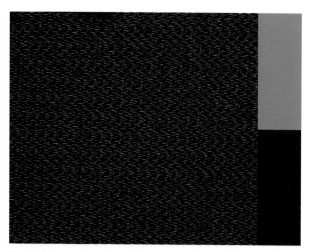

"C220" *by Maharam*
C220/10
Saran 81%, Polyester 19%

"Chant" *by Lulu DK*
Red
Cotton 100%

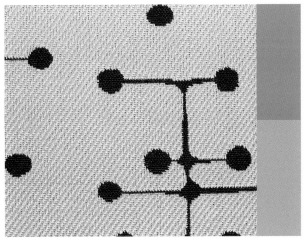

"Small Dot Pattern" *by Maharam*
Document
Cotton 71%, Polyester 29%

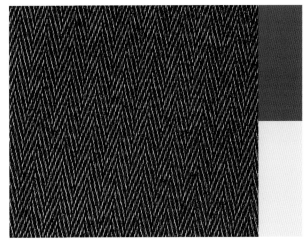

"C210" *by Maharam*
C210/1
Saran 82%, Polyester 18%

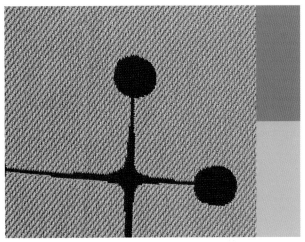

"Dot Pattern" *by Maharam*
Taupe
Cotton 71%, Polyester 29%

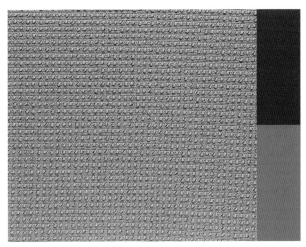

"Matrix" *by Pollack & Associates*
Granny Smith
Wool 92%, Polyamide 7%, Polyester 1%

"Salon" *by Maharam*
Dandelion
Wool 92%, Nylon 8%

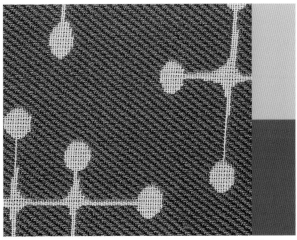

"Small Dot Pattern" *by Maharam*
Khaki
Cotton 71%, Polyester 29%

MODERN POP

Bold and graphic

Bold, graphic, bright, and playful, modern designs let fabrics take center stage. The bolder the color or print, the harder furniture and wall colors have to work to blend in, so be sure to choose fabric you really like. Many designers choose to restrict colors on accessories and furnishings to allow one brightly colored or wildly textured fabric to pop.

Modern fabric designs are often based on the world around us. An organic circle pattern may recall smooth, well-rounded stones in a river. A primary colored grid reflects the busy streets of the city. Exaggerated flowers come straight from a field of wild-flowers. These reflections, although several times removed and magnified, give us grounding to be able to live with and feel good about modern graphic design.

Modern fabrics push the boundaries of pattern, color, and texture, and incorporate high-tech, man-made materials and fresh takes on old favorites.

Modern fabrics, patterns, and designs are always one step ahead of the design world. Though longer lasting than a mere fad, modern is not yet classic, and, by the same account, not yet passé. These patterns and designs change with and reflect contemporary thought. Vintage modern designs take a look back at past patterns that have with-stood the test of time and won out as classic. Time-tested, classic modern fabrics can be combined with new, cutting-edge designs for a decorating range that will span the depths of innovative design from vintage Marrimekko to new Maharam.

OPPOSITE: When using bold patterns, minimize accent colors around them to keep a room from being overwhelmed. In this playful bedroom, red tulips and shiny apples provide the only color relief.

Decorating with Modern Fabrics

Modern fabrics can be intimidating, so it is wise to limit the patterns and colors in any given space. A grouping of bold prints in shades of the same color in a neutral room allows the patterns to play with one another without overwhelming. When decorating with ultrasaturated hues, such as lime green, fuchsia, poppy red, or tangerine orange, limit the surrounding colors. The color itself becomes the focus of the room. Often, a designer will use only black, white, and neutrals to play up bolder colors and patterns. This allows a plain-Jane room to take on a truly dramatic presence.

New man-made materials can do what other fabrics cannot. They can stretch like elastic, shine like patent leather, or twinkle like a starry night sky. Play up their abilities and show off their style by featuring them on a modern cube ottoman, flashy sofa, or sparkly window coverings.

In the end, when decorating with ultramodern materials, saturated colors, and over-the-top patterns, remember to have fun and maintain a sense of humor. Above all, allow these fabrics to take center stage.

BUILD THE LOOK

VINTAGE MODERN FABRICS CAN BE FOUND IN TAG SALES. LOOK FOR RETRO-PRINTED SCARVES AS A BASE FOR UNIQUE MODERN PILLOWS. TRY NEW FABRICS BASED ON VINTAGE DESIGNS FOR A FRESH TAKE ON MODERNISM.

OPPOSITE: Fabrics in playful, organic patterns and earth tones in sky blue, tangerine orange, and rich brown give a modern feel without being stark.

Tips for Decorating
with Modern Fabrics

✦ Bold, saturated colors can overwhelm a room, so choose a color you like and use it in a white, colorless room for maximum effect without dominating other elements. One bold piece of oversaturated neon color can make white walls glow with a subtle shading. For example, a bright fuchsia may make the white take on a pink or lavender hue, a subtle glowing effect echoed throughout the room.

✦ Bold abstract patterns tend to dominate other patterns, so are best used alone or accented with complementary solid colors. Oversized patterns for sofa upholstery and window treatments as a room's sole decoration can be dramatic. To keep a graphic pattern in check, choose color-ways in browns, whites, or black to accompany them. A sofa upholstered in a bold, circle design plays host to solid-colored accent pillows. Pair an eye-catching organic pattern with its opposite. A Modrian-inspired grid in primary colors contrasts and perks up a simply drawn circle pattern.

✦ The unique durability and eye-catching textures and colors of cutting-edge, man-made fabrics make them an attractive choice for heavily trafficked areas.

ABOVE: Feature a classic pattern in modern colorways for a contemporary take on a timeless look.

OPPOSITE: Striped pillows and throws in summery colors not only work wonders indoors but also create a refreshing outdoor room in a breeze. Add pillows and a coverlet to a bench for a refreshing reading spot al fresco.

Modern color palette

Contrast is the theme of the modern palette. Deep black and clean white accented with bright jewel tones create a crisp, modern look in design. Graphic colors such as bright red, orange, blue, and yellow make a modern statement that's hard to miss.

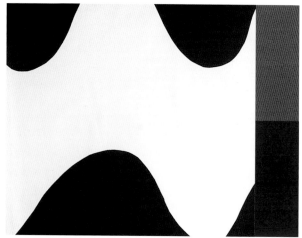

"Lokki" *by Marimekko*
Black/White
Cotton 100%

"Mixed Media" *by Knoll Textiles*
Titanium White
Polyester 56%, Cotton 27%, Polyurethane 17%

"Chant" *by Lulu DK*
Brown/White
Cotton 100%

"Simulate" *by Maharam*
Tear
Polyurethane 100%

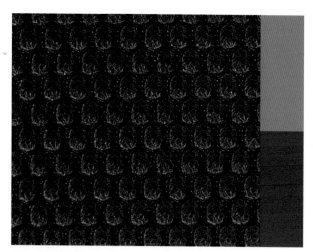

"Spacer" *by Jhane Barnes Textiles*
Blueberry
Polyester 100%

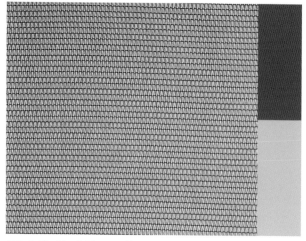

"Metallic Mesh" *by Knoll Textiles*
Nickel
Polyester 100%

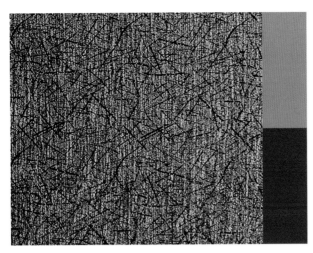

"Jetson Cloth" *by Home Couture*
Bronze
Cotton 56%, Polyester 27%, Viscose 17%

"Ceremony" *by Maharam*
Sense
Nylon 71%, Lycra 29%

"Method" *by Maharam*
Slate
Vinyl 93%, Polyurethane 7%

"3-D" *by Knoll Textiles*
Alpine
Polyester 48%, Rayon 33%, Acrylic 19%

"Alchemy" *by Pollack & Associates*
Gold
Viscose 41%, Cotton 36%, Polyester 23%

"Barbed Wire" *by Classic Cloth*
Charcoal
Polyester 43%, Cotton 34%, Silk 23%

Modern Fabric Combinations

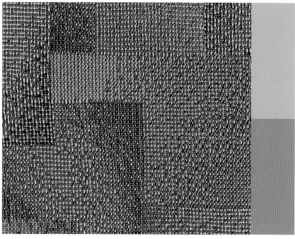

"Harvest Weave" *by Lee Jofa*
Groundworks
Cotton 100%

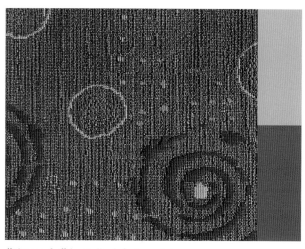

"Fireworks" *by Pollack & Associates*
Underbrush
Cotton 50%, Polyamide 22%, Linen 18%, Polyester 10%

"Icon" *by Lulu DK*
Brown
Cotton 100%

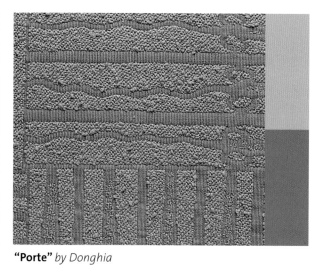

"Porte" *by Donghia*
Ash
Cotton 83%, Rayon 17%

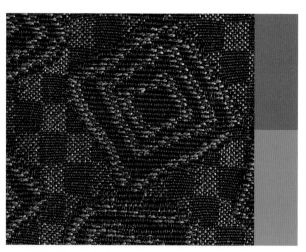

"Scrabble" *by Pollack & Associates*
Indigo
Cotton 82%, Viscose 18%

"Daria" *by Liberty Furnishings—Osborne & Little*
Gold/Blue
Cotton 100%

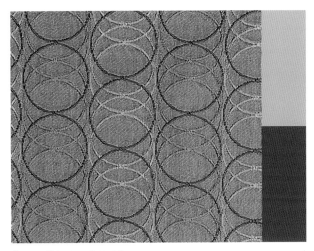

"Zoom" *by Knoll Textiles*
Chrome Green
Polyester 100%

"Mosaic" *by Knoll Textiles*
Caladium
Cotton 64%, Polyester 36%

"Stones" *by Knoll Textiles*
Granite
Cotton 54%, Polyester 46%

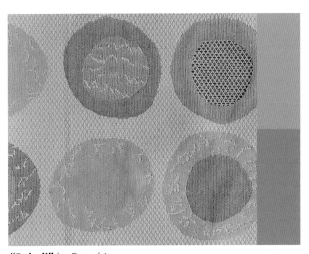

"Boboli" *by Donghia*
Sage
Cotton 59%, Viscose 41%

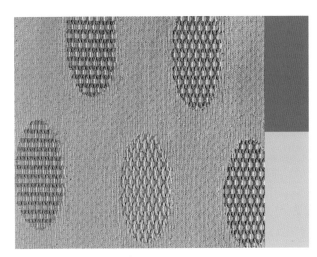

"Eclipse" *by Knoll Textiles*
Willow
Cotton 66%, Viscose 26%, Polyester 8%

"Odette" *by Liberty Furnishings—Osborne & Little*
Lavender
Viscose 65%, Cotton 35%

MODERN FABRIC COMBINATIONS

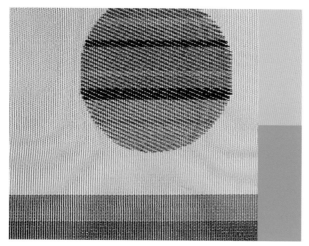

"Ondine" *by Liberty Furnishings—Osborne & Little*
Blue/Gold
Cotton 53%, Viscose 47%

"Clarkson" *by Robert Allen @ Home*
Blue
Cotton 100%

"Clarkson" *by Robert Allen @ Home*
Sage/Blue
Cotton 100%

"Unikko" *by Marimekko*
Red
Cotton 100%

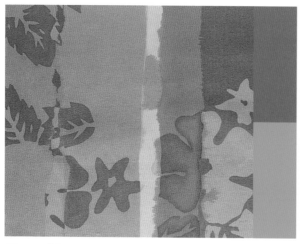

"Borneo" *by Pierre Frey*
Azur
Cotton 100%

"Silkkikukka Yellow" *by Marimekko*
Yellow
Acrylic 100%

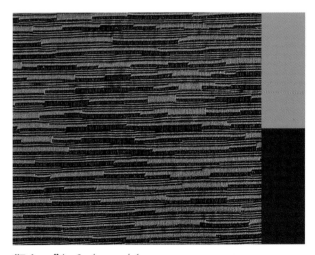

"Esprit" *by Knoll Textiles*
Fuchsia
Wool 80%, Nylon 20%

"Kaivo" *by Marimekko*
Blue/Black
Cotton 100%

"Lust" *by Pollack & Associates*
Black Satin
PVC 80%, Polyurethane 20%

"Saratoga" *by Jim Thompson*
Misty Moors
Silk 100%

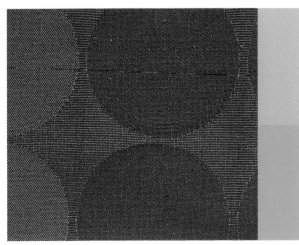

"Erina" *by Liberty Furnishings—Osborne & Little*
Red
Cotton 51%, Viscose 49%

"Taipan" *by Scalamandré*
Brindle
Cotton 100%

NATURE'S NATURALS

Inspired by the elements

Natural fabrics are derived from the raw materials available to Mother Nature herself. They are tough and resilient like earth and gently worn like a river stone. They are as breathable as mountain air and as flexible as bamboo in the wind. Washed cotton and raffia runners provide an elegant and durable dining room setting. Colorful soft linens or raw silks draped over a spare bed create a canopy with Zenlike elegance. Natural brown and natural green slipcovers in functional, sturdy canvas can easily move from the living room to the patio for al fresco entertaining.

From reedy window shades and earth-friendly hemp pillow covers to softly textured recycled upholstery, natural fabrics appeal both to those seeking clean, elegant lines and eco-conscious products. Recycled fabrics dyed with natural vegetable pigments have an added bonus as they provide a comfortably worn look and feel, as well as the opportunity to renew and reuse man- made products.

These fabrics are beautiful and sophisticated enough to work in an urban residence or simple and functional enough for a seaside cottage.

Natural fabrics work by bringing indoors the simplicity and beauty of the outdoors. An interior can be extended outside the boundaries of walls and windows, making an airy, cool, open environment. Colors are sky blue, grass green, yellow ochre, and sunset red. Patterns pay tribute to palm fronds, swirling clouds, and sandy beaches. Textures are gently woven, braided, and tied. Natural fabrics showcase the work of man and nature together at their best.

OPPOSITE: A crafted paper lantern imparts a warm glow to this Zen-inspired bedroom. Natural, undyed fabrics envelop a simple futon and are carried throughout in wall and floor coverings.

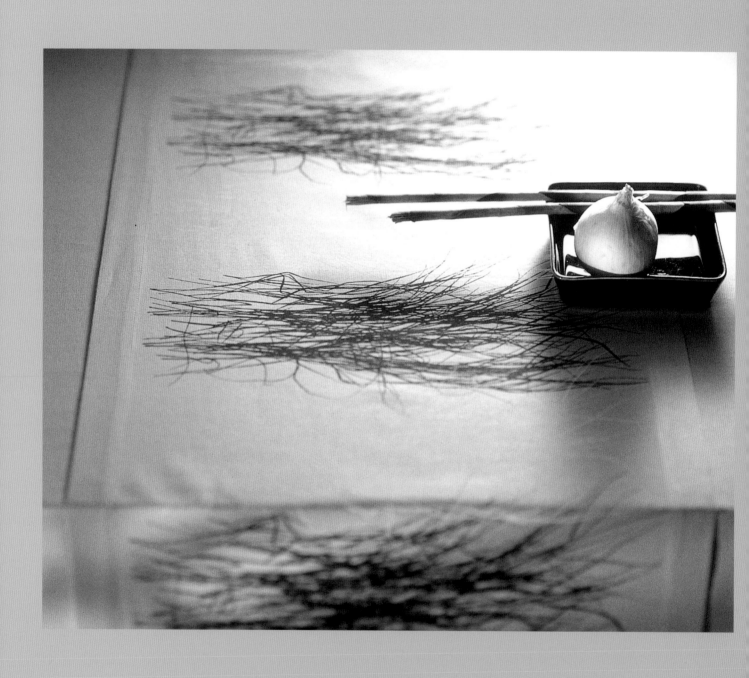

Decorating with Natural Fabrics

Although simplicity can mean unrefined, it does not have to mean unattractive. Natural fabrics work for people who want to bring a little of the outdoors in without sacrificing intelligent design. Neutral-toned fabrics and trim are, by nature, in the classic range and bring a clean look to any room of your home. From dining room to bedroom to terrace, natural fabrics can evoke the feeling of an open, airy space. Cool blues and greens or warm reds and oranges play off of neutral creams and browns to remind us of a refreshing breeze, cascading water, a brilliant sunset, or fresh earth.

Natural fabrics can be used in small or large quantities, as they are uncomplicated by excessively bold colors, patterns, or textures. Use them without reserve for a unified natural look. Begin with a blank canvas of hemp, stronger than both cotton and linen, for upholstery, bedding, or table linens. Brush on color with soft woven accents in reds and oranges or blues and greens. Choose simple, comfortable textures that will add contrast to the stiffer hemp for a balanced textural feel.

For an understated look, choose accents in nature-inspired patterns. Pillow covers, window treatments, and table-cloths printed with natural, sometimes whimsical, themes in neutral colors can temper a refined or formal classic look. Use these accents carte blanche in every corner.

BUILD THE LOOK

SELECT BASIC NEUTRALS SUCH AS CREAMY COTTONS, NATURAL LINENS, MUDDY BROWN HEMPS, OR CLAY-COLORED SILKS FOR UPHOLSTERY, BEDDING, AND WINDOW COVERINGS. ACCENT WITH COLORS INSPIRED BY NATURE. GRASS GREEN, SUNSET RED, SKY BLUE, AND YELLOW OCHRE ALL ADD SPLASHES OF EARTHY HUES.

OPPOSITE: A simple cotton table runner with a fresh grass design keeps a table setting clean and natural.

Tips for Decorating
with Natural Fabrics

✦ Like walking on a sugar sand beach, natural fabrics should feel good to the touch. Choose naturally caressing fabrics on upholstery and pillows. Unrefined linens, raw silks, and simple cottons look and feel at home from bedroom to living room.

✦ Go for more rugged fabrics—canvas, hemp, raffia, and sailcloth—where more durability is needed. These are perfect for table settings, window shades, and outdoor seating options. Recycled polyesters are resilient as well as earth-friendly and eco-savvy.

✦ Natural fabrics are flexible by nature. A simple white canvas slipcover is easy to make and can give a dining chair a fresh summer look or transform a plain garden chair into a fine dining seat.

✦ Natural fabrics are not necessarily rough and stiff. A canopy of diaphanous linen over a summery bed or billowing, gauzy curtains over a breezy window add a refreshing touch and the illusion of a seaside escape.

✦ A runner of woven raffia over a soft brown cotton tablecloth sets an earthy, Japanese-inspired table setting. Place-settings patterned with grass and bamboo are natural-born highlights

✦ Keep fancy trims to a minimum. Instead, use simple, clean fiber cording or piping on pillows and bedding, or try raffia ribbon, sea shells, or willow wreaths, gathered straight from nature, for curtain ties, pillow edgings, or napkin rings.

ABOVE: Try using thick, chunky weaves in unbleached fiber and colorways for a uniform natural look.

OPPOSITE: Use soft linen on every surface of a bedroom, from curtains to pillows to bedding, for a cool, uniform look and feel.

Natural color palette

A walk in the great outdoors will help you see the endless range of the natural color palette. This is a palette that encompasses every color of the rainbow—robin's egg blue, ocean green, new-growth green, and sunset yellow. These colors feel real, as if they have been ground from plants and earth.

Natural Fabric Combinations

"Martinique" *by Gretchen Bellinger*
Peach Beige
Wool 100%

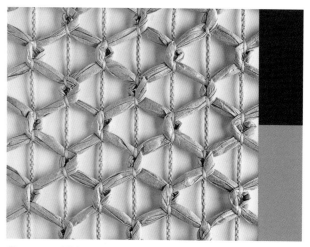

"Paperwork" *by Larsen*
Paperbag
Paper 80%, Polyester 20%

"Buzz Off" *by Donghia*
Linen
Cotton 100%

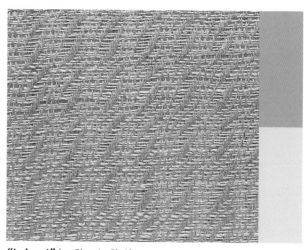

"Luisant" *by Classic Cloth*
Honeysuckle
Linen 68%, Silk 32%

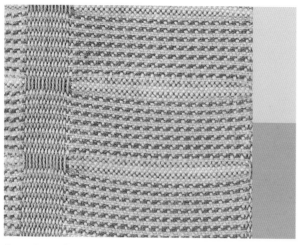

"Boathouse" *by Gretchen Bellinger*
Taupe/Dark Beige
Cotton 100%

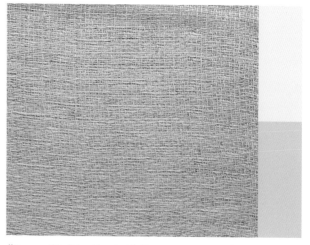

"Tranquility" *by Classic Cloth*
Natural
Linen 100%

"Hemp Linen" *by Rose Tarlow—Melrose House*
Sea Mist
Hemp 100%

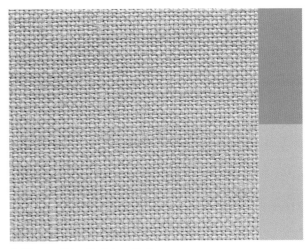

"Skimmer" *by Gretchen Bellinger*
Blue-Grey Gnatcatcher
Linen 100%

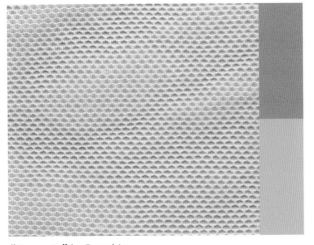

"Breeze In" *by Donghia*
Ivory
Cotton 100%

"Yachting Cloth" *by Gretchen Bellinger*
Clay
Cotton 100%

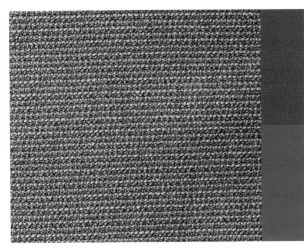

"Desert Sand" *by Sina Pearson Textiles*
Shale
Recycled Polyester 100%

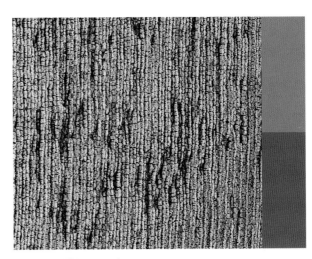

"Silkwood" *by Donghia*
Birch
Cotton 54%, Silk 46%

Natural Fabric Combinations

"Ebro" *by Knoll Textiles*
White
Wool 100%

"Desert Rocks" *by Sina Pearson Textiles*
Flint
Recycled Polyester 100%

"Skyline" *by Classic Cloth*
Dusk
Linen 100%

"Kilkenny" *by Classic Cloth*
Sherwood
Linen 74%, Worsted Wool 36%

"Butterfly" *by Sina Pearson Textiles*
Urania
Recycled Polyester 100%

"Akimbo" *by Gretchen Bellinger*
Sea Urchin
Cotton 100%

"Heirloom" *by Classic Cloth*
Ivory
Linen 88%, Cotton 12%

"Blanchard Stripe" *by Scalamandré*
Green & Beige
Cotton 100%

"Skiff" *by Gretchen Bellinger*
White
Cotton 100%

"Bruge" *by Classic Cloth*
Beeswax
Linen 100%

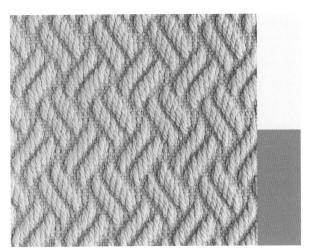

"Tisket a Tasket" *by Gretchen Bellinger*
Cane
Cotton 100%

"Pennine" *by Classic Cloth*
Lustre
Linen 100%

NATURAL FABRIC COMBINATIONS

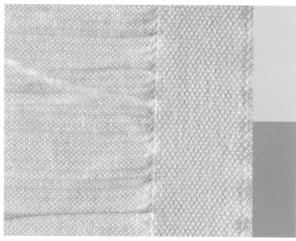

"Summerhouse" *by Gretchen Bellinger*
White
Cotton 100%

"Columba" *by Classic Cloth*
Wisp
Wool 72%, Cotton 20%, Polyester 8%

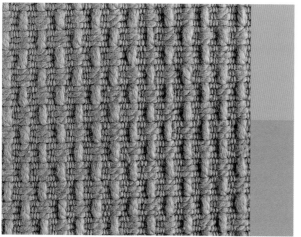

"Rowboat" *by Gretchen Bellinger*
Taupe/Grey
Cotton 100%

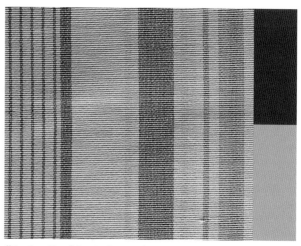

"Restoration" *by Scalamandré*
Green/Yellow
Cotton 100%

"Anne Bolyn Crewel" *by Scalamandré*
Whites
Linen 100%

"Arbois" *by Scalamandré*
Latte
Cotton 100%

"Botanica" *by Summer Hill*
Sea Grass
Cotton 88%, Linen 12%

"Bon Oeuf" *by Scalamandré*
Library Green
Cotton 100%

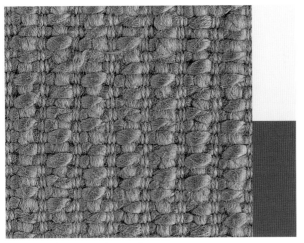

"Gibraltar" *by Gretchen Bellinger*
Sand
Cotton 100%

"Arum" *by Scalamandré*
Green/Taupe
Linen 70%, Cotton 30%

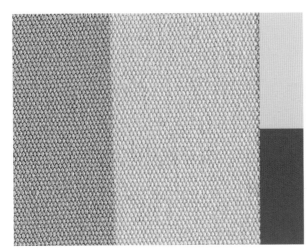

"Porch" *by Gretchen Bellinger*
Putty/Beige
Cotton 100%

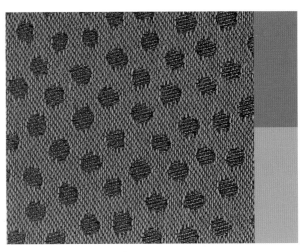

"Frog" *by Sina Pearson Textiles*
Tree Frog
Recycled Polyester 100%

SPRINGTIME FRESH

Light and airy, playful and elegant

Watery silks and sheer gauzes. Cotton madras and cool linen. These materials are as fresh as springtime, as light as a summer breeze, as delicate and colorful as a flower petal, and as shimmering as a reflection in a mountain lake.

Choose bright silks, linens, and gauzes for window dressings, bedding, and accents and feel the sun's rays waft in on a gentle breeze.

Airy fabrics reflect the outdoors and bring some of that feeling to any home, from city apartment to country manor. Like the scent of freshly washed linens hung out to dry, the clean coolness of a simple cotton seersucker, soft linen, or fresh percale whispers, "Slow down; linger a while." The coolest blue, palest pink, and most refreshing green pastels calm the spirit and soothe the eye without being dull.

Instead of simply providing privacy and hanging in a window, these fabrics breathe and move, diffuse light, and add an airiness to a room.

The bright, sheer nature of fresh fabrics gathers light and reflects it back to lift the mood in a room. Add metallic embellishments, such as a thin, golden pinstripe in a creamy cotton, or add iridescent color, as in a shimmering silk, and the light is bounced back and forth for an even greater sense of light play.

OPPOSITE: **A wall of windows framed by the sheerest of curtains allows light to filter onto a bed dressed in crisp, white linen and a cool blue bedside table for a truly refreshing retreat.**

Decorating with Fresh Fabrics

Bring the best of the outdoors in to create a quiet oasis. Light as air, these fabrics will not overwhelm a room, even when used in large measure. Draping a bed from floor to ceiling has a similar effect in a smaller space. Carry through the same fabric on the bedding, dust ruffle, and accent pillows for a hideaway from the world.

For more subtle highlights, use shining crystal and metallic accents on light-colored pillows to reflect light; many layers of complementary pastels on a single window for soft color; or a gauzy linen draped over an ornate chandelier for subdued, romantic lighting.

Fresh fabrics create the sense of a larger space by reflecting light. Open patterns on white backgrounds, barely discernable color on sheers, and bright, reflective colors in springtime shades keep the overall design of a room clean. Super sheer patterns and gauzy textured fabrics can be layered, sheers on sheers, sheers on cottons, or cottons on linens, for added depth and deeper color. The soft movement of these fabrics hung in a window or draped over an accent table or across a sofa adds color and life to a room.

BUILD THE LOOK

WRAP A ROOM IN PURE WHITE SHEERS IN PLACE OF WALLPAPER. A SHEER WRAP-AROUND CURTAIN WALL WILL SHIMMY AND SHINE, CREATING A HEAVENLY OASIS.

OPPOSITE: Stick with bright, open patterns and prints on a crisp white background for a classically clean, fresh look in the bedroom.

Tips for Decorating
with Fresh Fabrics

✦ Breathable and lightweight, the lightest cotton, simplest silk, and sheerest sheers are some of the best choices for a truly fresh feel. These materials provide lively movement in an open window, yet maintain privacy while allowing sunlight to filter in. Add metallic-printed pillows to play up natural light in dark corners. Layer several sheers of white with one or two layers of the sheerest of colors for subtle shading against light walls.

✦ Delicate fabrics, including watery silks, ultralight madras cottons, or sheer linens are the simplest, lightest fabrics around, so use them in places that won't require a fabric to take a lot of wear and tear. They are perfect for a sunny window, for accent pillows on a springy sofa, or for draping over a canopy bed for a summery feel. These fabrics are pure and elegant enough for a formal dining room, simple enough for a baby's nursery, soothing enough for a guest bedroom, and refined enough for a parlor room.

✦ Silks are luminous; they make color sing. One drawback, however, is that silk does not hold color well when exposed to light. When using silk in window treatments, be sure to line drapes or shades with a neutral backing. A liner will also provide added body for a super light silk. Or try using a swath of silk above the window line or wound around a chunky pole for color over the sheerest of sheer whites below.

OPPOSITE: For a quick bathroom refresher, choose springtime shades in cotton or linen, either of which will resist fading in humid environments, to cover a store-bought shower liner for a one-of-a-kind shower curtain.

Fresh color palette

Fresh colors are colors of spring and newness. Green dominates this color range in all its shades and tints. Cool green, with tropical blue, bursts with freshness, and matching soft pink with mint green almost has a taste. This color palette will bring any room to life.

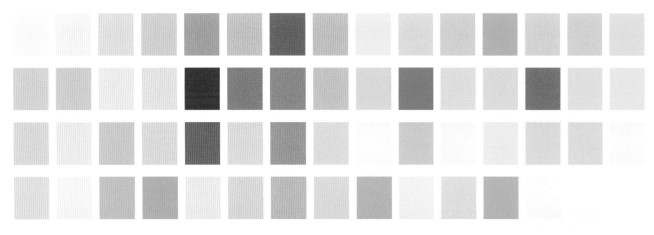

FRESH FABRIC COMBINATIONS

"Elise" *by Liberty Furnishings—Osborne & Little*
Sea Green
Viscose 80%, Linen 20%

"Rhumba" *by Gretchen Bellinger*
Flax
Cotton 100%

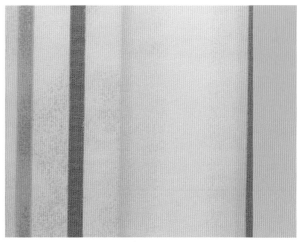

"Isadora" *by Liberty Furnishings—Osborne & Little*
Pink/Yellow
Viscose 70%, Polyester 30%

"Mercure" *by Creations Métaphores*
Rose de Tyr
Acetate 100%

"Similan" *by Jim Thompson*
Blue Harbor
Silk 100%

"Zap" *by Knoll Textiles*
Citronella
Polyester 100%

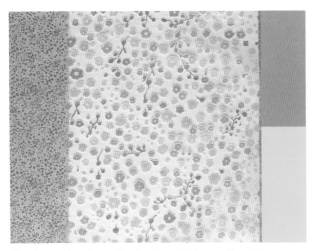

"Carlotta" *by Liberty Funishings—Osborne & Little*
Pink/Lavender
Cotton 70%, Polyester 30%

"Timour" *by Lorca—Osborne & Little*
Pink
Cotton 100%

"Armande" *by Liberty Furnishings—Osborne & Little*
Pink/Green
Viscose 60%, Cotton 40%

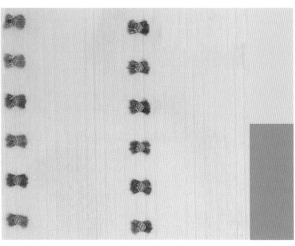

"Formal Wear" *by Pollack & Associates*
Spring
Silk 100%

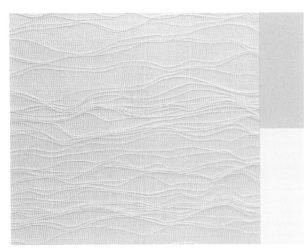

"Sea Lines" *by Gretchen Bellinger*
Crushed Coral
Silk 86%, Linen 14%

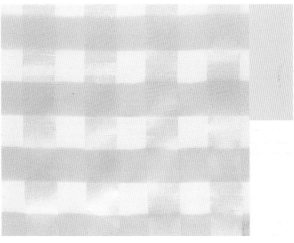

"Gossamer Plaid" *by Scalamandré*
Celadon/White
Silk 100%

Fresh Fabric Combinations

"Baldachine" *by Pollack & Associates*
Ice
Polyester 100%

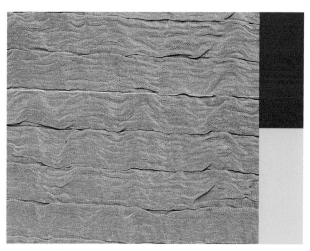

"Sylphide" *by Gretchen Bellinger*
Crystal Ball
Silk 100%

"Vista" *by Pollack & Associates*
The Blues
Cotton 75%, Silk 13%, Polyester 12%

"Daria Voile" *by Liberty Furnishings—Osborne & Little*
Blue
Viscose 70%, Polyester 30%

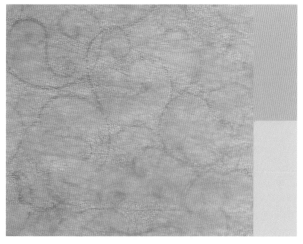

"Yseult" *by Creations Métaphores*
Ciel
Polyamide 100%

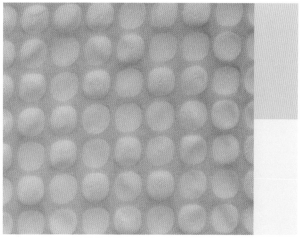

"Nimbus" *by Knoll Textiles*
Willow
Polyester 100%

"Savoir-Vivre" *by Pollack & Associates*
Ice
Silk 100%

"Opera" *by Creations Métaphores*
Ciel
Silk 40%, Acetate 60%

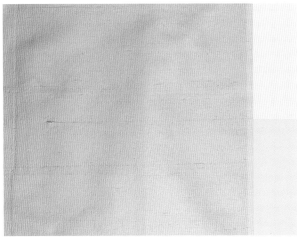

"Silk Stripe" *by Decorators Walk*
Pastels
Silk 100%

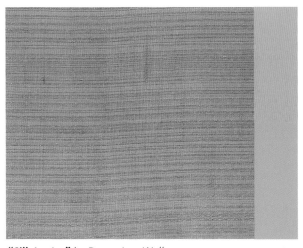

"Silk Lustre" *by Decorators Walk*
Ocean
Silk 75%, Polyester 25%

"Dew Drop" *by Gretchen Bellinger*
Pearl
Linen 100%

"Pure Silk Plaid" *by Decorators Walk*
Beige/Aqua/Tusk
Silk 100%

Fresh Fabric Combinations

"Fligts of Fancy" *by Gretchen Bellinger*
Champagne Sorbet
Silk 100%

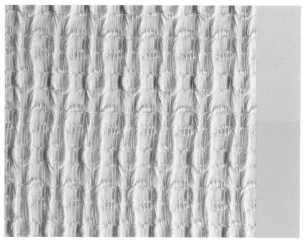

"Melody" *by Scalamandré*
Rose
Silk 100%

"Sugarcoated" *by Gretchen Bellinger*
Cane Sugar
Linen 100%

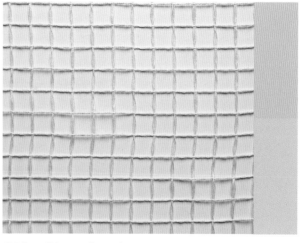

"Continuum Too" *by Larsen*
Pearl
Ramie 89%, Cotton 6%, Polyester 5%

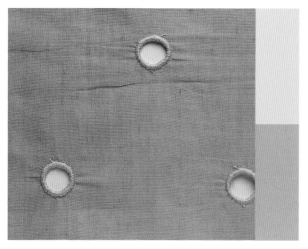

"Granita" *by Donghia*
Sky Blue
Cotton 98%, Polyester 2%

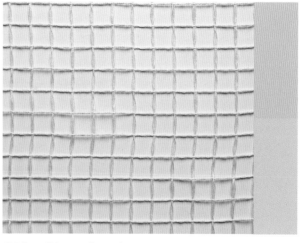

"Fishnet" *by Knoll Textiles*
Whitecaps
Polyester 100%

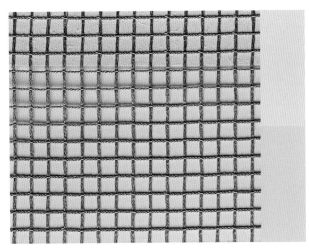

"Illusion" *by Classic Cloth*
Linen
Silk 56%, Polyester 44%

"Twinkle" *by Pollack & Associates*
Sky
Trevira Polyester 78%, Polyester 14%, Nylon 8%

"Tranquility" *by Classic Cloth*
Blanco
Linen 100%

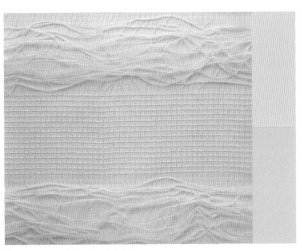

"Cats Meow" *by Rodolph Inc.*
A Whiskers White
48% polyester, 31% linen, 21% viscose

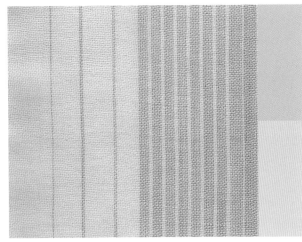

"Plaza Stripe" *by J. Robert Scott*
Ice Blue/Ecru
Wool 100%

"Moonshadow" *by Knoll Textiles*
Sky
Wool 54%, Polyester 46%

100% PURE

Versatile and wholesome

Looking for clean and unadulterated? Only 100% pure fabrics will do. Natural materials such as hemp, cotton, and wool show off the essential beauty of the fiber itself. One hundred percent silk reflects luminous color and feels fresh and light. It is perfect as luxurious window dressings. Linen in its pure state is crisp and cool, so it is at its best in the bedroom for elegant, cool bedding. Soft, warm, touchable wool makes a wing chair near a fireplace a cozy and restful retreat.

Fabrics of purity are simply comfortable, immensely versatile, and definitely beautiful.

Cottons, including colorful calicos, plush piled chenille, and elegant polished chintz, take on any task masterfully. Try color-saturated cottons in a garden room for a summery look year-round. Piled and woven hemps will be naturally strong, resilient, and super soft. Use them as simple slip-covers on outdoor chairs for a quick dining chair al fresco.

The simple textures and earthy color palette of pure fabrics have endless design possibilities, from creating a tranquil Zen mood in a dining room to a simple, restful atmosphere in a bedroom to a crisp, cleanly luxurious feel in a bath. Pure fabrics span the seasons from cool summery silks to warm winter wools. They need little trim, no extravagant color, and simple textures.

OPPOSITE: Subtle pattern gives neutrals depth and texture in a classically pure room with an overall white palette.

Decorating with
Pure Fabrics

Every room in the house is fair game for nature's finest. A felted wool feels cozy-casual on an oversized chair by the fire or fashion-formal on an ottoman in a masculine dressing room. A simple silk can be dressed up with tassels and trim for a formal window covering or played down on a plump pillow for a casual couch.

Pair pure fabrics in neutrals to temper other design moods. An undyed cotton slipcover is subtly exotic with a cinnamon cashmere throw. A white linen pillow sweetens a romantic, racy red bedcovering. A raw silk tablecloth becomes an expression of natural Zen beauty with a table runner of ecofriendly hemp.

Keep the color palate clean to play up the texture of pure fabrics. Classically clean, new neutrals—creamy white, sage green, or smoke blue—and pastels of the palest yellow or softest blue freshen a room and pair well with earth tones such as natural brown, russet red, and ocean blue.

BUILD THE LOOK

USE SIMILAR WEIGHT FABRICS WITH LIKE FABRICS FOR A UNIFORM FEEL. CHOOSE THE COOLEST COTTONS AS A MATCH FOR LIGHT SILKS. TRY WARM WOOLS WITH LUXURIOUS CASHMERE. KEEP IT NATURAL WITH ECO-FRIENDLY WOVEN HEMPS AND UNBLEACHED LINENS.

OPPOSITE: Pure silk curtains of cool sage green and creamy white drape beautifully and display their shine. Extra yardage on the curtains and matching tablecloth pool gracefully along the floor to create an ultraluxurious look.

Tips for Decorating
with Pure Fabrics

◆ Play up different incarnations of the same pure textile and display its differing weaves and piles for a subtle uniformity. A bed dressed up in cotton chenille bedspread and pillows, paired with the softest cotton sheets, gauzy pillows, and uncomplicated accessories, is transformed into a scrumptious, irresistible haven. Pure fabrics are naturals for bedding, relaxed seating, and casual accents, as they are supple and responsive to the touch.

◆ Smooth woven textures, like cotton, linen, and silk, add elegant grace to a formal table setting. Chunkier textures such as raw silk, wool, or woven hemps add subtle visual impact on large areas. Choose these for window treatments or upholstery.

◆ Hang a pure panel of gauze against a dramatic wall of mosaic glass tile, a hard floor of poured concrete, or panels of heavily textured wood to lighten stark modern architectural lines. Be sure to hang the fabric from the ceiling and allow it to billow and pool on the floor for the ultimate in simplicity.

◆ A simple Japanese shoji screen of pure cotton linen is as ethereal as it is functional, hiding a cluttered corner with clean elegance or turning a bare loft apartment into a simply sophisticated, multiarea abode.

OPPOSITE: One hundred percent cotton never looked so pretty and fresh as in this bedroom setting. Cotton is versatile, lightweight, and inexpensive, so it can be used from floor to ceiling for a total, lasting look of purity.

Pure color palette

Colors in their purest form make up this range. What you see is what you get. Basic blues, clean reds, and soft neutrals will embellish a pure décor without overwhelming it. Colors have low contrast, and are soft and subtle, with nothing added.

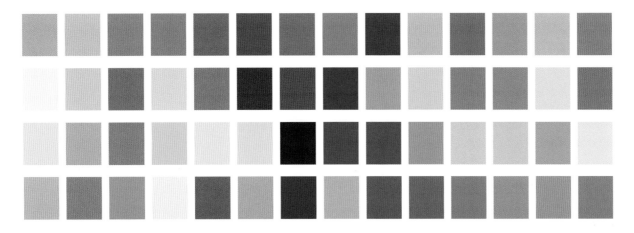

Pure Fabric Combinations

"Reflection" *by Classic Cloth*
Fawn
Silk 100%

"Palasa" *by Osborne & Little*
Natural
Linen 100%

"Pennine" *by Classic Cloth*
Golden
Linen 100%

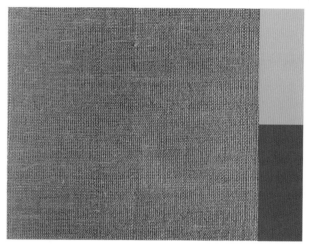

"Silk Tapis" *by J. Robert Scott*
Ice Blue
Silk 100%

"Zen Cloth" *by Home Couture*
Sprig
Cotton 100%

"Hemp Linen" *by Rose Tarlow—Melrose House*
Saffron
Hemp 100%

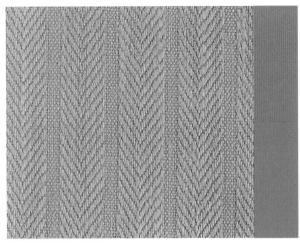

"Canterbury Stripe" *by Rose Tarlow—Melrose House*
Butternut
Hemp 100%

"Harewood Handblock Print" *by Lee Jofa*
Nectar & Sage
Linen 100%

"Skyline" *by Classic Cloth*
Sunset
Linen 100%

"Serenity" *by Classic Cloth*
Natural
Worsted Wool 100%

"Plaza Sheer" *by J. Robert Scott*
Ice Blue
Wool 100%

"Spring Garden" *by Classic Cloth*
Daffodil
Chintzed Cotton 100%

Pure Fabric Combinations

80

"Kashmir" *by Classic Cloth*
Nutmeg
Cashmere 100%

"Folio" *by Larsen*
Sand
Wool 100%

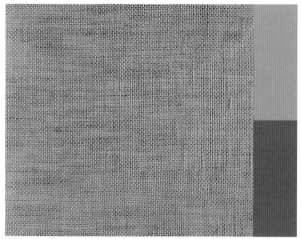

"Isle Cloth" *by Home Couture*
Sea
Linen 100%

"Kaeki Beach" *by J. Robert Scott*
Ice Blue/Snow
Cotton 100%

"Chanvre" *by Classic Cloth*
Portland
Hemp Pile 100%

"Fabulous Cloth" *by Home Couture*
Vapor
Wool Crepe 100%

"Bonard" *by Scalamandré*
Gold
Silk 100%

"Gainsborough" *by Decorators Walk*
Natural
Linen 100%

"Linen Scrim" *by Groundworks—Lee Jofa*
Ecru
Linen 100%

"Oxford Silk Stripe" *by Lee Jofa*
Cream
Silk 100%

"Pure Silk Stripe" *by Decorators Walk*
Aqua/Pink/Tusk
Silk 100%

"Madeleine Silk" *by Decorators Walk*
Ivory
Silk 100%

Pure Fabric Combinations

"Wildflower" *by Pollack & Associates*
Sunlight
Silk 100%

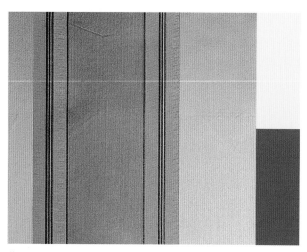

"Federal Stripe" *by Scalamandré*
Gold
Silk 100%

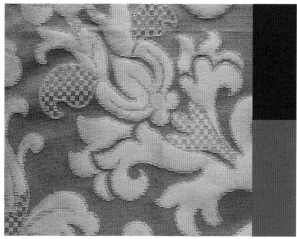

"Ancestral Damask" *by Lee Jofa*
Gilt
Silk 100%

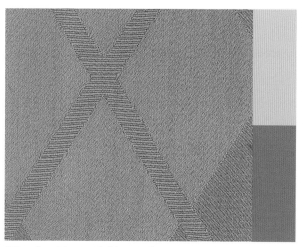

"Merging Diamonds" *by J. Robert Scott*
Ice Blue
Wool 100%

"Renaissance" *by Classic Cloth*
Dove
Cotton 100%

"Canon Check" *by J. Robert Scott*
Ice Blue/Ivory
Silk 100%

"Patong" *by Jim Thompson*
Tropic Tan
Silk 100%

"Serafina" *by Groundworks—Lee Jofa*
Creme
Silk 100%

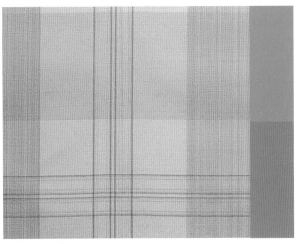

"Turandot Plaid" *by Scalamandré*
Chartreuse/Beige
Silk 100%

"Taffeta" *by J. Robert Scott*
Ice Blue
Silk 100%

"Zanzibar" *by Pierre Frey*
Beige
Cotton 100%

"Icon" *by Lulu DK*
Grey Blue/Light Blue
Cotton 100%

COUNTRY CHARM

Pretty, classic, and comfortable

Simple. Bucolic. Country is down-home familiar. Bright, cheerfully colored denims, checks, ginghams, and stripes are easy to mix and match and feel just as comfortable on a porch as in a more dressed up eat-in kitchen. A classic country pattern, such as wide hunter green-on-white stripes, can even make its way to covering a formal dining chair.

Country fabrics are durable and mostly washable and color fast. They work inside or out: as curtains in a sunny kitchen window, as fresh cushion covers on a wicker porch chair, or as a pretty tablecloth in a dining room, breakfast nook, or sunroom.

The simplest of textures, from smooth cotton percales to worn denims, and the cheeriest of patterns, from easy stripes and checks to those nature-inspired, afford an ultraclean, country fresh look and feel.

Lively and practical, these fabrics are by no means boring or plain. Naturals with a well-worn, relaxed hand—simple cottons, linens, or hemp, to name a few—fit the bill. Be creative; recycle textiles that may already be on hand. From tea towel curtains to quilt pillow covers and wall hangings, country makes the most of every piece.

LEFT: Country fabrics are durable and mostly washable. Dress your breakfast nook in a cheery country print to set the mood for a delicious meal.

OPPOSITE: Pretty cotton fabrics in crisp red-and-white patterns create a clean country bedroom with romantic appeal.

Decorating with Country Fabrics

Simple, understated, and practical describes these fabrics, but don't be fooled. They are bright, cheerful, and colorful. The country palette runs the gamut from sunflower yellow to sky blue, barn red, and grass green. Patterns are graphic and simple—checks, stripes, and tiny floral prints.

Country can lead multiple lives, moving from the front porch to the kitchen or from the bedroom to the backyard. A canvas stripe in natural and hunter green makes a comfortable, durable seat that is stylish enough to move from the front porch rocker to a kitchen chair. A home-made quilt can combine with crisp white linens for a pretty bed setting or do double-duty as a delightful picnic blanket.

Country fabrics are best suited for casual settings, as they remind us of simpler times and a more casual, family-centered home. Their bright, sunny colors and fresh patterns make family members as well as guests feel truly at home.

BUILD THE LOOK

COMBINE COLOR OPPOSITES IN UNIQUE PASTEL SHADES AND PATTERNS, FROM SPRING GREEN PLAID TO LAVENDER GINGHAM TO SHERBET ORANGE STRIPES, FOR A MODERN TAKE ON TRADITIONAL COUNTRY. A WICKER SOFA LINED WITH AN ARRAY OF GINGHAM CHECKS IN SEVERAL DIFFERENT PASTEL COLORS SOON BECOMES FAVORED SEATING.

ABOVE: Combine garden shades of marigold yellow, grass green, strawberry red, and bluebell blue in different patterns for a sunny country effect. Match gingham checks and pretty stripes with nature-inspired prints for added contrast and energy.

OPPOSITE: Cabinet curtains in garden shades of sunflower yellow and spring green are an easy way to cheer up a kitchen and a convenient solution to hiding an under-the-counter storage area.

Tips for Decorating
with Country Fabrics

✦ On beddings, incorporate well-worn fabrics such as a quilted matelisse or antique linens for an open airiness. Recycle handmade, lace-trimmed linen napkins from dining room table to bedroom pillow covers. A plain handkerchief is a simple, inexpensive backing.

✦ Quilts. The ultimate in handmade country. Whether antique or newly made, these versatile works of art play many roles in a single room: a colorful bed hanging or an eye-catching cover for a bed, bolster, or pillow; a cozy furniture throw or a treasured wall hanging. Quilts can live several lives from generation to generation.

✦ To keep a country look from appearing too plain, use checks or stripes, for example, in bright primary colors on a whiter-than-white background. The brilliant colors of blue denim, deep red cotton, or bright yellow linens are natural companions and can be used together in any proportion. Accent a solid red window seat cushion with matching red pillows in checks, stripes, and toile prints for a sunny reading corner. Add solid white pillows and trim all in simple red piping for a clean, consistent look. Combine denim blue and red calico in a kitchen widow valance with ultrasimple pleating for a pretty framed effect. Bring together ink blue and sunny yellow on tablecloths, napkins, and placemats for a classic color combination.

✦ Trims and accessories can turn a plain, neutral pillow or window covering from stuffy to simply country. Pretty country trims, such as white eyelet lace on baby bumpers, comforters, and pillows, lend an old-fashioned heirloom look. Pintucks on pretty cotton bedroom pillows add a delicate feminine touch. Adorn pillows with buttons, from tiny to oversized, for a unique, homemade look.

OPPOSITE: Denim, in a lighter weight, shows its softer side in a simple checked bed curtain. Pair this curtain with simple white cotton sheets and matching color details for a classic country look.

Country color palette

Egg-yolk yellow and apple red are the core of the traditional country palette, and mixed with classic greens and blues, the farm-fresh feeling is easy to create. Simple red checks and ceramics accented in blue are country style essentials.

COUNTRY FABRIC COMBINATIONS

"Country Plaid" *by Decorators Walk*
Natural
Cotton 76%, Linen 24%

"Kilkenny" *by Classic Cloth*
Steel
Linen 74%, Wool 26%

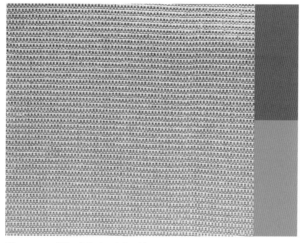

"Ipanema" *by J. Robert Scott*
Ice Blue
Cotton 60%, Silk 40%

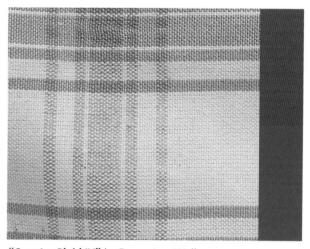

"Country Plaid IV" *by Decorators Walk*
Natural
Cotton 84%, Linen 16%

"Monterey" *by Decorators Walk*
Soft Blue
Cotton 100%

"Giotto" *by Classic Cloth*
Blue Stone
Linen 100%

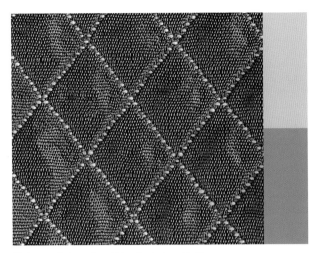

"Channel Crossings" *by Gretchen Bellinger*
Blue Blood
Polyester 60%, Cotton 40%

"Brittany Stripe" *by Scalamandré*
Indigo
Cotton 100%

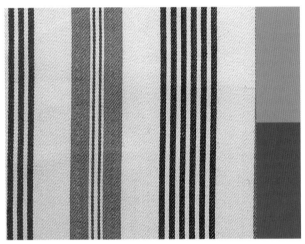

"Yosemite" *by Decorators Walk*
Red/White/Blue
Cotton 100%

"Canvas Cloth" *by Rose Tarlow—Melrose House*
Mottled Blue
Hemp Canvas 100%

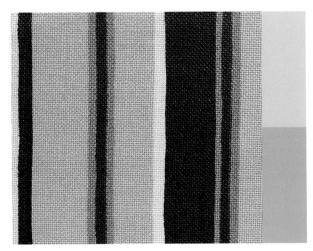

"Catwalk" *by Lulu DK*
Light Blue/Brown
Cotton 100%

"Fougere on Hessian" *by Old World Weavers*
White/Natural
Jute 100%

Country Fabric Combinations

"Susan" *by Scalamandré*
Sky/Marina Blue
Viscose 56%, Cotton 44%

"Handspun" *by Jim Thompson*
Wedgwood
Cotton 100%

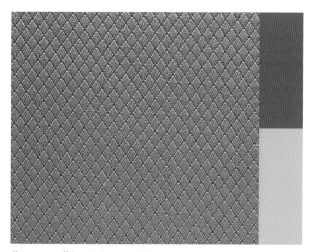

"Trapunto" *by Scalamandré*
Blue
Cotton 100%

"Cabourg" *by Pierre Frey*
Blue
Cotton 100%

"Cassis" *by Pierre Frey*
Blue
Cotton 100%

"Bandanna" *by Oilcloth International*
Red
Printed Vinyl

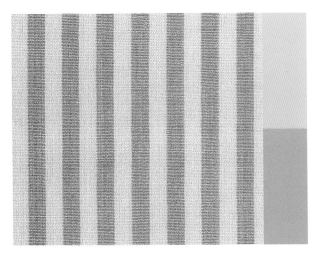

"Dilly Stripe" *by Scalamandré*
Azure/White
Cotton 100%

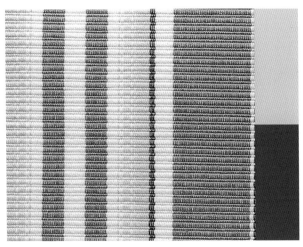

"Bedford" *by Decorators Walk*
Blue/Yellow
Cotton 93.5%, Polyamide 6.5%

"Bonnie Plaid" *by Scalamandré*
Yellow/White
Cotton 58%, Silk 42%

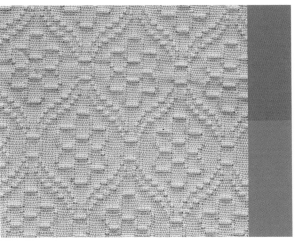

"Langston" *by Scalamandré*
Golden Rod
Cotton 100%

"Ashley" *by Decorators Walk*
Black
Cotton 100%

"Glen Plaid" *by Oilcloth International*
Black/White
Printed Vinyl

COUNTRY FABRIC COMBINATIONS

"Tralee" *by Classic Cloth*
Penny
Linen 57%, Worsted Wool 43%

"Gallo Macchia" *by Scalamandré*
Florentine Gold
Cotton 100%

"Diamante" *by Scalamandré*
Maize
Cotton Chenille 100%

"Catherine Matlasse" *by Lee Jofa*
Cloud
Cotton 100%

"Coronation Bouquet" *by Scalamandré*
Robin's Egg Blue
Cotton 100%

"Imperial Check" *by Decorators Walk*
Pink
Rayon 63%, Polyester 37%

"Tick Tick" *by Decorators Walk*
Leaf
Cotton 100%

"Fete Champagne Trellis" *by Scalamandré*
Red/Gold/Blush
Cotton 100%

"Giotto" *by Classic Cloth*
Terra Cotta
Linen 100%

"Mapleton Cloth" *by Home Couture*
Fig
Llama 51%, Wool 49%

"Lulu" *by Scalamandré*
Yellow/Multi
Cotton 96%, Rayon 4%

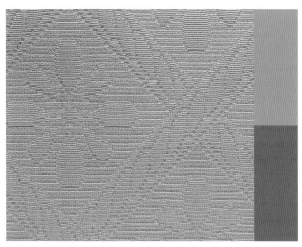

"Regimental Cord" *by Scalamandré*
Lettuce Green
Cotton 69%, Rayon 31%

SENSUAL ROMANTICS

Flirtatious and delightful

Whether creating a flirtatious retreat with floor-to-ceiling toile de Jouy or with a blushing glimpse of pastel pink cushions on a caramel colored couch, romantic fabrics can evoke the softer side of life or excite our senses and awaken our passions.

By engaging each of the five senses in turn, romantic fabrics create visual delight, a cozy retreat, or a flirtatious turn of whimsy. Soothe the eye with cool pastels, warm ruby reds, and dreamy creams. Cozy up to lightweight velvets, comfortable cottons, and light-as-air sheers. These tantalizing textures will make you want to touch them again and again. Tease the taste buds with luscious chocolate browns, cotton-candy pinks, and sugary ice blues. Stop and smell the floral scents of roses and lilacs. Listen to the trickle of a cool mountain stream, the effervescence of bubbly champagne, and the whisper of a billowy white cloud.

From bright, colorful flower prints to delicate depictions of classic romantic scenes, romantic fabrics invite, embrace, tease, tickle, and flirt. They are touchably soft, classically crisp, or delicately sheer. Tones range from muted mauve to robin's egg blue to rosy reds. So what really makes a romantic fabric romantic? Like a fragrant bouquet of flowers, a deliciously decorated cake, or a beautiful spring day, they are just plain pretty.

Delicate pastels and racy reds; rich velvety and silky textures; and lacy, floral, feminine patterns are the essence of the romantic design.

ABOVE: Use delicate sheers to filter light to create a romantic glow in any room. Combine soft fabrics with wall color for a warm and seamless look.

OPPOSITE: A table setting becomes intimate and romantic when set against the deepest ruby red, as on these thick velvet curtains, and accented with masses of richly shaded roses as a centerpiece.

Decorating with Romantic Fabrics

ABOVE: Pile on the romance with accent pillows of lush satin and metallic prints. The shine of pretty pinks and golds will entice you into luxury.

BUILD THE LOOK

ROMANTIC HUES TRANSFORM STATELY STRIPES INTO SHEER POETRY. TRY COMBINATIONS OF CHOCOLATE BROWNS AND ROSY REDS, FLOWERY PASTELS AND THE WHITEST WHITES, METALLIC SHIMMERS OF GOLD AND SILVER, OR HEAVENLY SHADES OF SKY BLUE AND CLOUD PINK.

Romance can be fun and flirtatious or passionate and steamy. So, too, can decorating with these poetic fabrics. Use them coquettishly, sparingly, to lend a sense of humor, a feminine touch, or a brightness to an interior. Pretty pink piping, baby blue buttons, and lavender pleated ruffles dress up neutral toned pillows, draperies, bedding, and tablecloths without going overboard.

For a bolder look, have a passionate love affair with a romantic fabric such as a luscious toile and drape it from floor to ceiling. The richest velvety reds and purples and lusciously silky pinks and icy blues push the limits to the extreme. Pull out all the stops. Pool drapery and table coverings on the floor; accent with gold metallic or sparkly trimmings; and cover every piece of furniture with luxurious, touchable fabrics.

Whether using romantic fabrics modestly or lavishly throughout the home, some rules remain the same: soften harsh lines with ruffles, piping, and lace; block out unsightly views and filter harsh light with pretty panels of filmy sheers; brighten dark corners with sparkly trims and bright champagne gold and white; and temper dominant pieces with draping throws to compose a restful haven that no one will ever want to leave. Fall in love with romance and tuck it into every corner of the house.

OPPOSITE: Romance isn't always red hot. Introduce pretty pastels with romantic floral or toile de Jouy patterns for a young, innocent look.

Tips for Decorating
with Romantic Fabrics

✦ Make a date for decorating a room. Think pretty, soft, feminine, and inviting.

✦ Introduce candlelight for a tranquil glow. Add luminous highlights of warm creamy whites and golden champagne tones. Add trimmings of sequins, metallics, and beads to play up the shimmer. At the windows, layers of delicately veiled sheers in pale pastels block out harsh sunlight and unaesthetic views.

✦ A romantic room should be luxuriously comfortable. Pile pretty pillows on pillows in every corner of a room, each in a variety of dreamy floral patterns or feminine shades for ultimate comfort. Throw brightly colored velvets on a deep-toned, velvety, plush chaise for an irresistible nook. The shine of a pretty polished cotton pillow covering in a sweet floral pattern makes a smartly tailored sofa even more of a show-off. Accent with touchably soft washed linen and cotton broadcloth pillows in neutral tones for a smart, classically romantic look.

✦ Plant a garden of flowers with patterns that have an eye to the seasons. For a spring garden look, stick with roses, lavender, or tulips on a light linen slipcover. For fall, go for sunflowers, dahlias, or ivy on sturdy cotton pillows, bolsters, and throws.

✦ For the ultimate in romantic luxury, use captivating toile patterns as wallpaper and cover a room from floor to ceiling. This look works especially well in a small enclosed room, making a cozy and elegant space even more intimate. Carry the toile through to accent pillows and window treatments for a total look.

OPPOSITE: You don't need to be an expert seamstress to add a bit of romance to a bedroom setting. Simply drape a pretty eyelet lace over two bamboo poles suspended from the ceiling for an ultra-romantic canopy.

Romantic color palette

The romantic colors stem from sensual red but present softer, quieter versions of this arousing color. The bright side of this palette will elicit a passionate energy to an interior, and the soft side, a sweet embrace.

Romantic Fabric Combinations

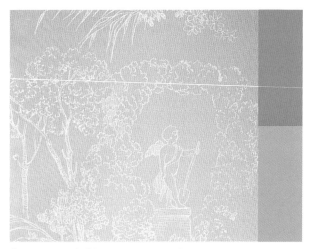

"Organza Toile" *by Decorators Walk*
Ecru
Silk 100%

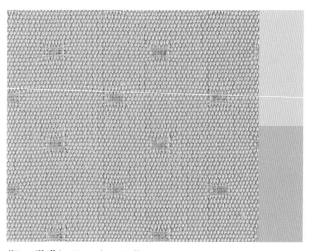

"Pastille" *by Gretchen Bellinger*
Anise
Cotton 62%, Rayon 38%

"Ciro Damask" *by Decorators Walk*
Palace Pink
Silk 60%, Rayon 40%

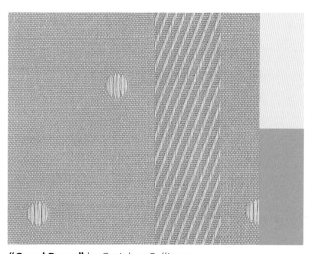

"Grand Dame" *by Gretchen Bellinger*
Cameo
Wool 42%, Polyester 40%, Silk 18%

"Marriage of Figaro" *by Decorators Walk*
Celadon
Cotton 100%

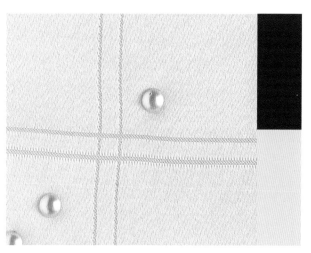

"Diva" *by Gretchen Bellinger*
Pearl/White
Silk 100%

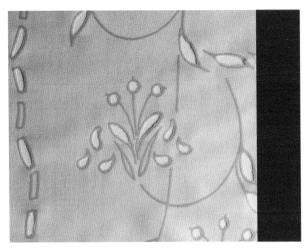

"Madeira" *by Scalamandré*
Swan
Silk 100%

"Silk Lustre" *by Decorators Walk*
Melon
Silk 75%, Polyester 25%

"Colombine" *by Decorators Walk*
Rose Pink
Silk 100%

"Kate" *by Scalamandré*
Yellow
Viscose 85%, Cotton 15%

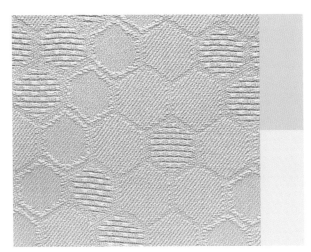

"Queen Bee" *by Gretchen Bellinger*
Bisque
Silk 100%

"Ingrid" *by Scalamandré*
Plum/Cream
Cotton 68%, Viscose 32%

Romantic Fabric Combinations

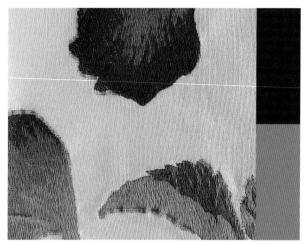

"Alma Rose" *by Lorca—Osborne & Little*
Red
Cotton 72%, Viscose 28%

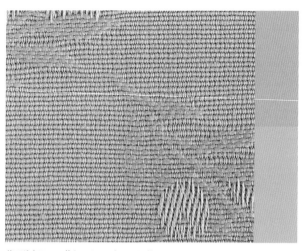

"Wild Berry" *by Gretchen Bellinger*
Coffeeberry
Cotton 58%, Viscose 42%

"Stand Alone" *by Gretchen Bellinger*
Ivory Tower
Polyester 100%

"Spring Garden" *by Classic Cloth*
Cameo
Cotton 100%

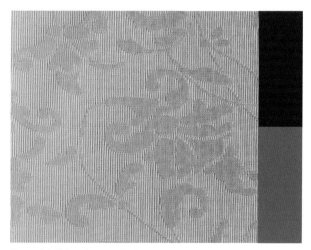

"Ismelda" *by Classic Cloth*
Sand
Cotton 40%, Viscose 33%, Silk 27%

"Glazed Over" *by Gretchen Bellinger*
Honey Glazed
Cotton 100%

"Sutara" *by Osborne & Little*
Wine/Gold
Silk 60%, Linen 40%

"Isana" *by Osborne & Little*
Green
Silk 100%

"Love Bird" *by Scalamandré*
Melon/Bronze
Silk 100%

"Isana" *by Osborne & Little*
Gold
Silk 100%

"Damasc Villa Erba" *by Classic Cloth*
Rosemary
Cotton 71%, Silk 29%

"Laluka" *by Osborne & Little*
Ruby
Silk 100%

Romantic Fabric Combinations

"Eugenie" *by Scalamandré*
Green/Cream
Silk 100%

"Jour de Juin" *by Scalamandré*
Multi/White
Silk 100%

"Chadwick" *by Decorators Walk*
Blue
Cotton 100%

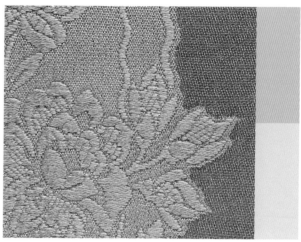

"Garlands" *by Gretchen Bellinger*
Pink/Beige
Silk 100%

"Tulleries de Jourdain" *by Scalamandré*
Pink on Cream
Cotton 100%

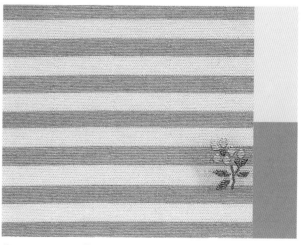

"Forget-Me-Not" *by Gretchen Bellinger*
Periwinkle
Silk 100%

"Caprice des Dames" *by Scalamandré*
Multi / White
Silk 100%

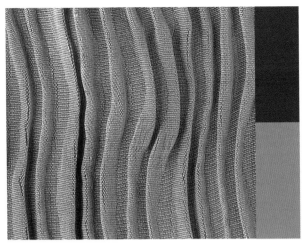

"Isadora" *by Gretchen Bellinger*
Malama
Silk 100%

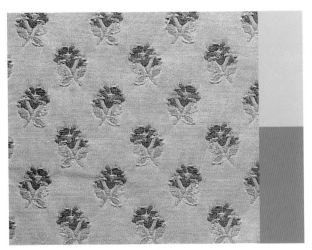

"Jacqueline Weave" *by Lee Jofa*
Teal
Cotton 51%, Viscose 49%

"Chinoiserie Staircase" *by Lee Jofa*
China Blue
Cotton 100%

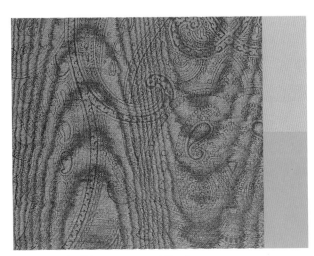

"Salamandre" *by Creations Métaphores*
Brume
Acrylic 51%, Rayon 49%

"Carlotta Lampass" *by Lee Jofa*
Jewel
Cotton 60%, Viscose 40%

ANCIENT EXOTICS

Colorful, mysterious, spiritual, and luxurious

Exotics are the traditional fabrics and patterns of those countries traversed along the silk trading route, from China, across India and ancient Persia, to Turkey and the Mediterranean. Voluminous shimmering silks, colorful linens, and sensual saris, seemingly from off a camel's back. Jewel tones of emerald, sapphire, and ruby red and spicy shades of cinnamon and saffron from colorful bazaars. Ancient paisley prints and embroidered and woven patterns from ancient harems. Exotic fabrics reach back into the mysterious past and conspire to ravish the senses and re-create the mystery.

The only rule here is to pile on the luxury wantonly. Exotic fabrics romance the soul, seduce the senses, and transport us to another time and place.

Lush saris, draped across windows, wash a room with a veiled glow. Intricately patterned pillows and heavily mirrored wall hangings create an inviolable and intimate space. Jewels of color, which deepen the luxurious feel, bathe the silks, warm cashmeres, soft linens, and diaphanous gauzes inviting hours of hedonistic lounging.

Exotic fabrics work best in rooms meant for luxurious entertaining or mysterious and romantic interludes. Ancient paisley prints and intricately embroidered patterns playfully entice and add visual depth as accent pillows. Crystal and mirrored trimmings provide sparkle and light, tempering the deepness of the richest earth tones.

ABOVE: Drape thick drapery across doorways to muffle sounds and create a feast for the eyes with intricate patterns of red and brown.

OPPOSITE: Draping a bedroom corner from floor to ceiling with shimmering fabrics, lush trims, and mirrored accents, reminiscent of those from along the ancient silk trading route, creates a sinfully exotic retreat.

Decorating with Exotic Fabrics

Steal some of the splendor of the ancient silk road with the materials they traded: sumptuous silks in saffron and cinnamon; carefully embellished tapestries to adorn the settees of kings and queens; flirtatiously feminine saris reminiscent of those adorning beautiful harem girls; and magical woven materials to drape the tented floors of shahs. When decorating with exotic fabrics, do not be afraid to use a heavy hand. The more that is piled on, from floor pillows to tented ceilings, the more mysterious and intimate the atmosphere that is created.

For an even more extravagant look, turn a living room into a canopied harem complete with draped walls, pillows upon pillows, sumptuous upholsteries, and luxurious accents. Accents should be heavily adorned and strewn like treasured jewels in a king's coffers. Glittering mirrors and metallic trims keep the look from becoming too dark. Solid colors allow rich, complicated patterns to pop.

For just a hint of the exotic, drape a simple silk sheer in saffron to filter the afternoon sun, add silky pillows in pastel paisleys on chaise lounges, sofas, and chairs, or use a softly woven ethnic rug as a colorful focal point in a neutral-toned room.

BUILD THE LOOK

EXOTIC FABRICS HAVE THE MOST IMPACT WHEN THEY ARE LAYERED, DRAPED, ALLOWED TO POOL ON THE FLOOR, USED IN PILLOWS AND CUSHIONS, AND FLUNG LAVISHLY OVER FURNISHINGS.

ABOVE: A table setting becomes intimate and exotic when set with the deepest ruby red, as with this lush tablecloth and napkins.

OPPOSITE: Piles and piles of pillows in spicy shades of cinnamon, curry, mustard, paprika, and cumin create an overall warm palette to an otherwise neutral room.

Tips for Decorating
with Exotic Fabrics

✦ Conceive an exotic, incredibly luxurious romantic space. Drape thick velvet or heavy embroidered drapery across doorways to muffle sounds. Hang walls with beautiful draping fabrics or woven rugs for an intimate tentlike feel. On windows, drape silky sheers in glowing earth tones to diffuse an amber glow throughout the room. Line a deep red window shade in yellow ochre to recall kingly banners on display.

✦ Fashion a feast for the eyes with intricate patterns in deep jewel tones. Rich brown, red, and green paisleys and printed cottons play well against a sofa or chaise uphol-stered in a thick velvet green or blue. Incorporate exotics in small doses with softer splashes of earth tones. Try draping a deep orange panel of the softest silk over a dark wood dining table for an exotic pashalike meal.

✦ Mimic the traders' caravans with a base of camel brown on a seductively curved chaise and drape it with crimson, gold, and blue throws. Trim pillows with silken tassels, flickering mirrors, and delightful susurrus bells.

✦ All fabrics should invite languorous lounging. Soft cotton chenille takes on a different life when patterned with paisleys. Put touches of softness everywhere for an enveloping feeling of comfort.

✦ Pair a naturally faded, vegetable-dyed wool rug with giant silken floor pillows for luxurious extra seating. Allow table and window coverings to flood the floor with extra long lengths, showing that you have spared no expense when outfitting your castle or tent. Contrast dark woods with bright, rich fabrics for an even more intimate glow.

OPPOSITE: **Try using an antique embroidery piece that may be too fragile for upholstery as a special wall hanging. This chair finds a place of honor, framed by the delicately embroidered piece behind it. The intricate cuts of the chair legs and back mimic the pattern of the wall hanging to create a harmonious pairing.**

Exotic color palette

The colors of distant lands and dreams of grandeur, this palette favors gold and jewels. Luxurious and over the top, exotic colors are daring reds and oranges, golden yellows accented with emerald green and sapphire blue. A bold palette for the adventurous decorator.

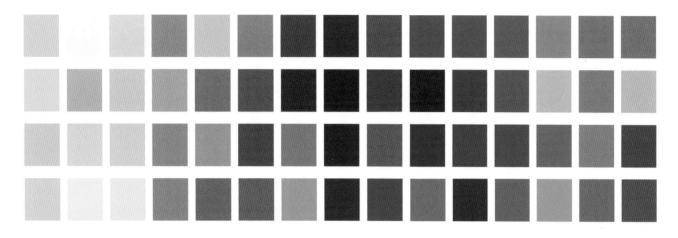

Exotic Fabric Combinations

"Casting Illusions" *by Gretchen Bellinger*
Ginger Sparkle Larvae
Cotton 50%, Polyester 50%

"Limousine Cloth" *by Gretchen Bellinger*
Maserati Mustard
Wool 100%

"Zouk" *by Osborne & Little*
Multi
Cotton 60%, Linen 40%

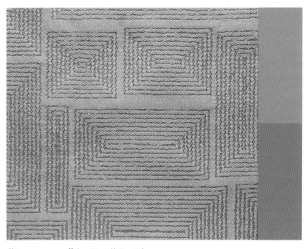

"Campagna" *by Knoll Textiles*
Ginger
Cotton 66%, Polyester 34%

"A Cut Above" *by Gretchen Bellinger*
Topaz
Rayon 51%, Cotton Pile 49%

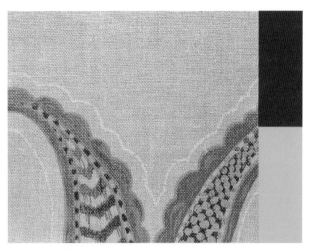

Palampore" *by Osborne & Little*
Teal/Gold
Linen 100%

"Zap" *by Knoll Textiles*
Flash
Polyester 100%

"In the Clouds" *by Gretchen Bellinger*
Tea Smoke
Polyester 64%, Cotton 36%

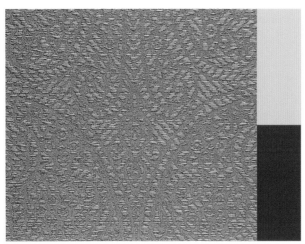

"Jivala Silks" *by Osborne & Little*
Teal/Gold
Silk 100%

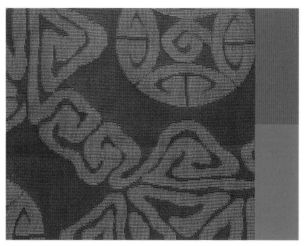

"Omen" *by Donghia*
Divine Red
Cotton 59%, Viscose 26%, Polyester 15%

"Viceroy Velvet" *by Pollack & Associates*
Midnight
Mohair Pile 100%

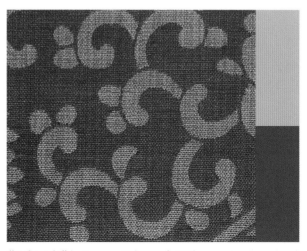

"Golconde" *by Lorca—Osborne & Little*
Spice
Cotton 46%, Viscose 28%, Linen 14%, Polyamide 12%

Exotic Fabric Combinations

"Live Wire" *by Gretchen Bellinger*
Phosphorescent
Mohair Pile 100%

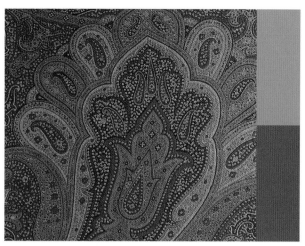

"San Remo Silk Paisley" *by Lee Jofa*
Ruby
Silk 100%

"Viceroy Velvet" *by Pollack & Associates*
Curry
Mohair Pile 100%

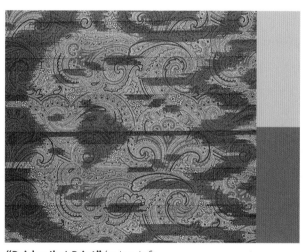

"Paisley Ikat Print" *by Lee Jofa*
Ochre
Cotton 100%

"Spread Your Wings" *by Gretchen Bellinger*
Golden Teal
Silk 100%

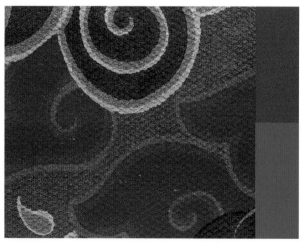

"Khor" *by Lorca—Osborne & Little*
Multi
Cotton 100%

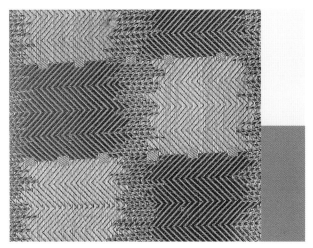

"Brinker" *by Scalamandré*
Leaf Green/Taupe
Silk 100%

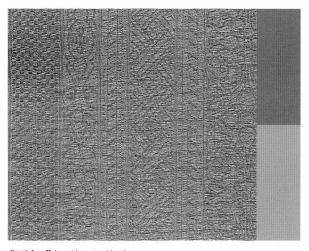

"Midas" *by Classic Cloth*
Oro
Cotton 41%, Viscose 33%, Silk 16%, Metal 10%

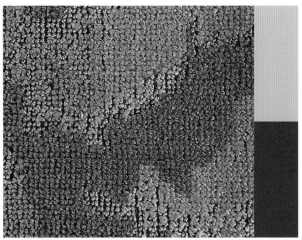

"Tiepolo" *by Pollack & Associates*
Mancha
Viscose 72%, Cotton 20%, Polyester 6%

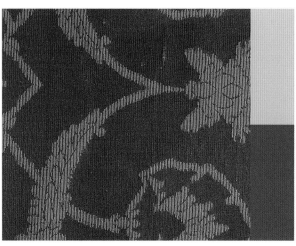

"Florissant" *by Scalamandré*
Gold on Garnet
Silk 100%

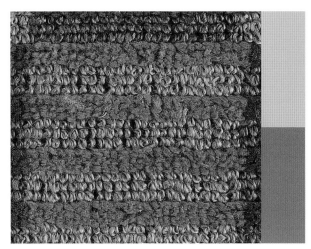

"Tribal Check" *by Pollack & Associates*
Saffron and Rosewood
Linen Pile 100%

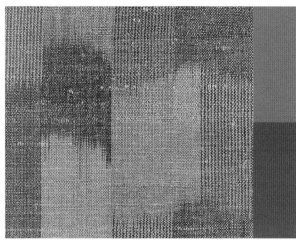

"Jahlal" *by Scalamandré*
Gold, Copper, Rose
Silk 100%

Exotic Fabric Combinations

"Kendi" *by Classic Cloth*
Kanxi
Wool 60%, Silk 40%

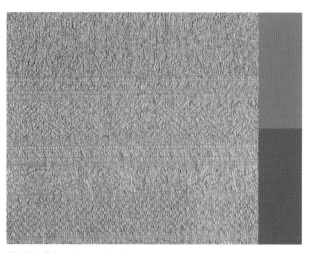

"Midas" *by Classic Cloth*
Gild
Cotton 37%, Acetate 27%, Silk 14%, Metal 8%

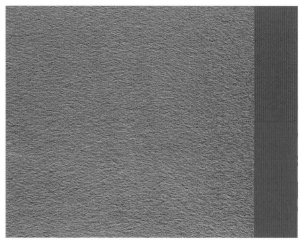

"Kashmir" *by Classic Cloth*
Sesame
Cashmere 100%

"Luminesce" *by Classic Cloth*
Cinnabar
Silk 60%, Cotton 40%

"Una" *by Knoll Textiles*
Persimmon
Nylon 72%, Elastin 28%

"Tearose" *by Classic Cloth*
Caraway
Cotton 52%, Polyester 38%, Lurex 10%

"Bambous Myesterieux" *by Jacques Bouvet et Cie*
Berry
Cotton 100%

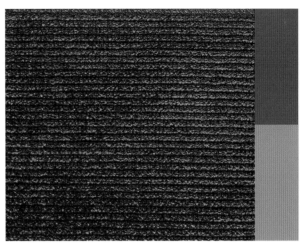

"Milieu" *by Classic Cloth*
Lava
Linen Face 100%

"Yang Tze" *by Scalamandré*
Black
Cotton 53%, Silk 47%

"Renaissance" *by Classic Cloth*
Cinnabar
Cotton 100%

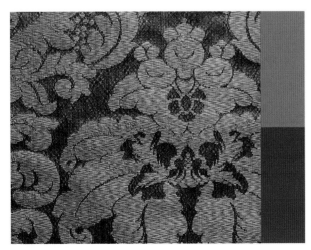

"Lucia" *by Scalamandré*
Bristol Blue
Silk 100%

"Turkish Delight" *by Pollack & Associates*
Saffron
Cotton 48%, Silk 39%, Polyester 13%

SUBTLE REFINEMENT

Sophisticated and elegant

The best of the best without going over the top, refined fabrics know when to say when. They deliver sophisticated styles, colors, and textures with just the right amount of restraint. Monochromatic brocades and damasks provide flat texture and intricate pattern for a subtle impact on walls, furnishings, and window hangings. Polished draped silks offer whisper-soft texture and color sheen. Refined fabrics provide a subtle contrast to highly polished, ornate wood pieces and reflect the shimmery feel of gilded furniture. They will not overwhelm a room and, thus, are the perfect choice for a space with unique furnishings or a spectacular view.

These genteel fabrics, with their color, shine, texture, and pattern, impart a quiet, understated elegance.

Refined fabrics provide muted, neutral colors, from warm creams to earthy reds and mossy browns, as well as crisp highlights, such as cobalt blue, golden yellow, and emerald green; subtly shaded patterns, including stripes, herringbone, and classic florals; and widely varying textures, from brocades to tweeds, all of which highlight the integrity of the fabric.

A peachy, striped silk smartly shows itself off as a window treatment. A whispery blue brocade offers a soothing shade of texture for a formal dining room. A sophisticated floral chintz reflects the intricate beauty of an antique gilded armchair.

OPPOSITE: Limiting colorways in this living room to two rich colors, amber and maroon, with attention to intricate patterns and detail, keeps a refined decor simple.

Decorating with Refined Fabrics

ABOVE: Drape a room in brocades to create a polished and refined look. Muted colors and subtle patterns make a room look formal and well put together.

Refined fabrics add charm and sophistication, without being overly stuffy or overwhelmingly ornate. Take brocades, cotton chintz, or simple silks and make any room look polished and well put together, top to bottom. Shimmering light, muted color, and subdued pattern and texture are the essence of their overall elegance and grace. Temper heavy furniture: Try a softly toned floral chintz on an ornately carved antique sofa and trim with a delicate neutral piping for a contemporary take that is not too modern.

Refined fabrics may be best suited to more formal rooms but can easily make the transition to less formal settings. A sunny buttercream silk on a sumptuous bedroom chaise, a sophisticated accent pillow on a comfortable navy wing chair, or a smart valance in a sunny breakfast nook all lend a subtle charm. The addition of more elaborate trims—gold cording, tassels, and deep pleats—transform these casual treatments into formal attire.

BUILD THE LOOK

COMFORTABLE TEXTURES SUCH AS HERRINGBONE, CORDUROY, AND WAFFLE CHECKS BLEND IN WELL WITH GOLDEN COLOR PALETTES AND WITH WELL-WORN ANTIQUE FURNITURE. A HOME LIBRARY TAKES ON A SCHOLARLY TONE WITH A CLASSIC HERRINGBONE DESIGN ON A TOBACCO COLORED, WOOL-UPHOLSTERED READING CHAIR.

OPPOSITE: A gathering of plump brocade pillows lined up and sitting at attention reflects a group of silver collectables set for afternoon tea.

Tips for Decorating
with Refined Fabrics

✦ Damasks and brocades, with their flattened textural patterns and their subtle shadings and feel, work splendidly as wall coverings. Find a pattern with two tones of the same color, say a soft rose and an icy pink, and then use the base color for accents and accessories to gain symmetry and balance within a space.

✦ The softer the shade of a silk, the more the texture of the silk will be featured. A warm cream, cool ice blue, or shimmering pale pink will allow the luminescent quality of the silk to shine without drawing extra attention to it. These hues are perfect for a subtle silken window treatment in a relaxed bedroom or as an accent table topper in a drawing room.

✦ Cotton has its place in a refined setting as well. Small, smartly patterned calico prints give an overall impression of pattern without dominating. Use them anywhere, from pillows on a solid colored sofa, a slipcover on an affordable easy chair, or linens on a simple table.

✦ Crisp linen hand towels trimmed in delicate Battenburg lace, piled in stacks or draped on towel rods for guests, transform a guest bathroom into a refreshing one that pampers friends and family.

OPPOSITE: The classic color combination of blue and gold keeps a subtle, Asian-inspired pattern looking fresh and sophisticated.

Refined color palette

Refined colors are elegant and sophisticated. Soft and subtle, they make a statement without shouting.
These colors are found on the entire range of the color wheel but are mainly subtle shades of classic colors.

Refined Fabric Combinations

"Ascot" *by Donghia*
Hyacinth
Cotton 57%, Silk 22%, Polyester 21%

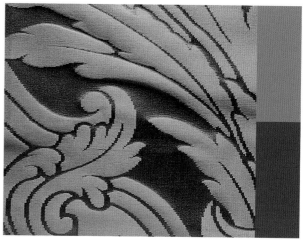

"Damasc Villa Erba" *by Classic Cloth*
Borage
Cotton 79%, Silk 29%

"Ranong" *by Jim Thompson*
Celestial
Cotton 70%, Silk 30%

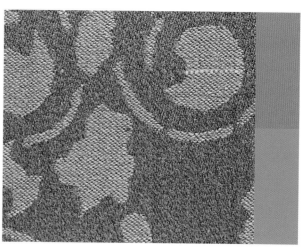

"Celtic Damask" *by Classic Cloth*
Linen
Silk 70%, Linen 30%

"Louise" *by Pierre Frey*
Bourgeon
Viscose 56%, Cotton 44%

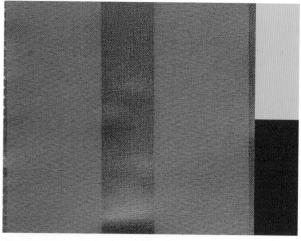

"Antigua" *by Creations Métaphores*
Caroubier
Acrylic 52%, Rayon 48%

"Jarvis" *by Jim Thompson*
Sky Cloud
Silk 80%, Polyester 20%

"Mystic Plaid" *by Jim Thompson*
Highland Gray
Silk 100%

"Stoddard" *by Scalamandré*
Red
Cotton 79%, Silk 21%

"Shangri-La Damask" *by Lee Jofa*
Bronze
Silk 70%, Wool 30%

"Italian Damask" *by Decorators Walk*
Teal
Silk 60%, Rayon 40%

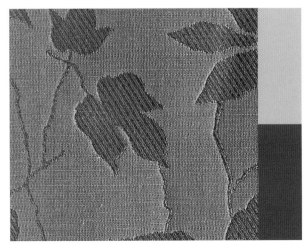

"Liana" *by Pollack & Associates*
Earth and Sky
Silk 40%, Linen 20%, Wool 20%, Cotton 20%

REFINED FABRIC COMBINATIONS

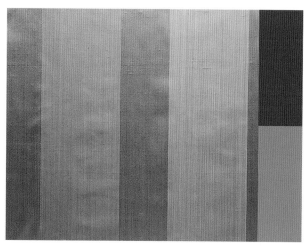

"Damasco Sienese" *by Scalamandré*
Mist Grey/Blue Strie
Silk 100%

"Rigoletto Stripe" *by Scalamandré*
Tan/Chartreuse/Amber
Silk 100%

"Newport Damask" *by Scalamandré*
Eggshell
Silk 100%

"Millbrooke Stripe" *by Cowtan & Towt*
Sky
Silk 40%, Wool 39%, Linen 21%

"Sargent Silk" *by Cowtan & Towt*
Sea Glass
Linen 70%, Silk 30%

"Gainsborough" *by Decorators Walk*
Apricot
Linen 100%

"Pesce" *by Classic Cloth*
Rosemary
Silk 70%, Linen 30%

"Coach Cloth" *by Maharam*
Heath
Wool 100%

"Mosaique" *by Classic Cloth*
Sage
Cotton 52%, Viscose 48%

"Silhouette" *by Pollack & Associates*
Celadon
Viscose 51%, Cotton 49%

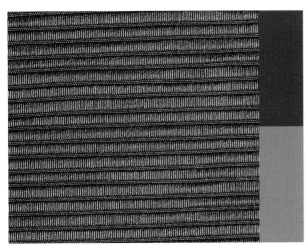

"Grand Otto" *by Classic Cloth*
Rosemary
Cotton 70%, Rayon 30%

"Basillo Damask" *by Decorators Walk*
Endive
Linen 100%

REFINED FABRIC COMBINATIONS

"Into the Woods" *by Pollack & Associates*
Portobello
Cotton 60%, Linen 24%, Polyester 16%

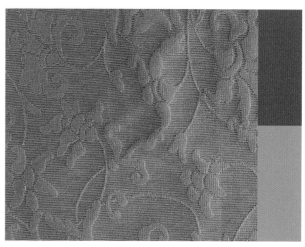

"Ismelda" *by Classic Cloth*
Adobe
Cotton 40%, Viscose 33%, Silk 27%

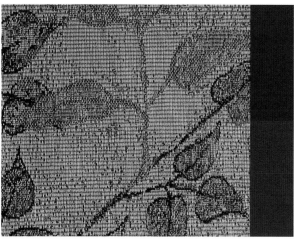

"Chaya" *by Donghia*
Beige
Cotton 54%, Wool 42%, Polyester 3%, Nylon 1%

"Compagna" *by Scalamandré*
Strawberry/Beige
Cotton 51%, Viscose 49%

"Chevron" *by Classic Cloth*
Blush
Wool 87%, Cashmere 9%, Nylon 4%

"Castlegate Weave" *by Lee Jofa*
Indigo
Cotton 74%, Viscose 17%, Nylon 9%

"Temptation" *by Pollack & Associates*
Peanut
Viscose 58%, Cotton 29%, Polyester 16%

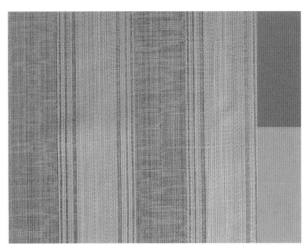

"Documentary" *by Scalamandré*
Pink/Red/Brown
Linen 100%

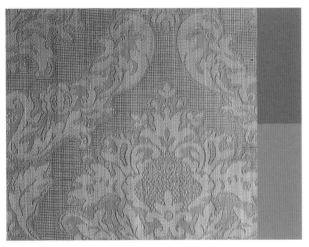

"Bellagio Strie Weave" *by Lee Jofa*
Biscuit
Cotton 75%, Rayon 25%

"Menlo Moire Stripe" *by Lee Jofa*
Antique Green
Viscose 59%, Rayon 41%

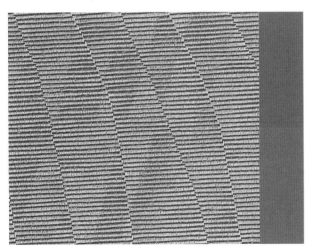

"Kaleidescope" *by Donghia*
Fool's Gold
Viscose 40%, Cotton 36%, Linen 24%

"Luca" *by Scalamandré*
Green/Yellow
Linen 100%

ROYAL LUXURY

Soft and rich

If luxurious fabrics could be summed up in three words, those words would definitely be "feel good fabrics." The color palette combines rich, jeweled shades of emerald, ruby, and sapphire with the deepest earth tones of russet brown and yellow ochre. Luxurious gold and silver metallic fabrics, trims, and accents add sparkle and highlight. Opulent textures invite the touch, from the slinkiest of silks, to the warmest of quality wools and cashmeres, to the plushest of velvets. Patterns are deeply intricate, finely embroidered, and carefully woven.

Fabrics have been used for centuries to create lavish effects and to display wealth. Affluent travelers would bring with them intricate embroideries, royal brocades, and rich tapestries to prove their status. Vintage and antique tapestries can still be found; grace delicate areas with these as wall hangings or pillow covers. Machine-made tapestry provides a more economical and durable option for special areas, such as on elegant dining chairs, delicate footstools and ottomans, or as an off-season fireplace screen.

A delight to the eye and to the touch.

Sometimes thick, sometimes richly textured, always sumptuously soft, carefully woven silks, cashmere blends, and linens invite the touch. For a bit of the palatial, pile wools, mohair, silky velvets, or chenille on sofas, chaise lounges, deep chairs, pillows, or places where the feel of the piece is all-important. Silk beddings of different weights conjure up a magical haven. Soft, quality linens for table settings and in guest bathrooms make guests feel like royalty.

OPPOSITE: **A ruby red bedroom setting incorporates a range of textiles, from the finest silk and linen to brocade and velvet, in different shades of the deepest red for a rich romantic boudoir.**

Decorating with Luxurious Fabrics

Your home is your palace, so lavish it in pure luxury. Pamper yourself with the deep textures, jewel-like color, and rich patterns of these fabrics. Pile a sofa with velvet pillows in every jewel like shade, from emerald green to wine red, from cobalt blue to Egyptian gold. Hang windows with the most luminous of golden silks, lined with thick linen to add weight and body. Allow them to pool on the floor for the ultimate in royal treatments. Adorn walls with the immensely intricate handwork of antique and contemporary tapestries to absorb sound and add regal warmth. Embellish every surface with elaborate trims. Heavy golden tassels, thick braiding, tiny jewels, and deep pleats add extra luxury to window treatments, pillows, tablecloths, and upholstery. Surround yourself with the best of the best. Allow yourself to sink into the world of decadent decorating.

BUILD THE LOOK

FOR A CHIC LOOK, PILE ON THE LUXURY. LAYER PLUSH VELVETS, CASHMERE BLENDS, AND SILKY CHENILLES FOR A SINK-IN HORIZONTAL LOUNGING IN RELAXED GATHERING ROOMS.

OPPOSITE: Several fabric types in the deepest shades available combine for a seductive richness. Here, the sofa is decked out in wool and silk upholstery, accent pillows are covered in the softest velvets, and the curtains display a heavy tapestry design.

Tips for Decorating
with Luxurious Fabrics

◆ Infuse your home with a bit of luxury. Velvet curtains hung just inside the front door bring rich color to a foyer and block bright light in summer and cold wind in winter. Dark, heavy velvets provide the longest-wearing piled material, and work superbly as upholstery and blackout draperies. Voluminous silk window treatments in gold brighten a formal living room. Tie back plain polished cotton curtains with a colorful strip of silk for a touch of elegance in the kitchen.

◆ Scatter wool pillows and cashmere throws to cozy-up a formal couch. Adorn guest baths with the finest linens. Try using antique napkins as special hand towels. A stack of beautiful linens makes guests feel truly at home. Line the bottom of dresser drawers with antique linens in natural colors to protect lingerie and sweaters in a unique way.

◆ Add elaborate trims to plain surfaces for a quick luxurious fix. Tassels smarten up curtains and do double duty as elegant tiebacks. Oversized taffeta bows in deep jewel tones attached to simple canvas slipcovers make chairs fit for the most formal dining room.

◆ Create your own wall hanging by framing intricate tapestries, either antique or newly made, to add texture to a dull space. Hang larger fabric squares or rugs of intricately embroidered fabric above a dark wood bed for a rich bedroom den. Resurrect antique or show off new machine-made tapestry fragments by making them into pillow coverings, using a plain, durable backing.

ABOVE: Pamper yourself with texture, color, and pattern. Pile pillow of lush satin and Egyptian gold to create a corner of luxury.

OPPOSITE: Exquisitely adorned pillows in royal shades of purple and gold turn a delicately carved antique settee into a rich, colorful showpiece.

Luxurious color palette

Luxury calls for deep color. Midnight blues, ruby reds, and emerald greens are the palette of luxurious living. Combined with soft creams and whites, this palette begs to be touched.

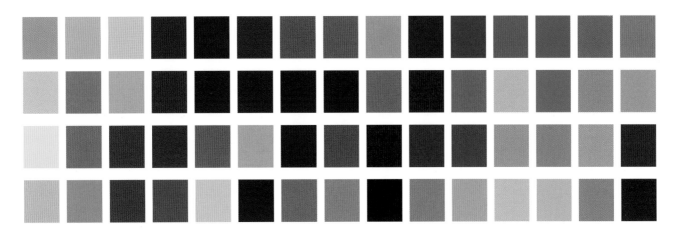

LUXURIOUS FABRIC COMBINATIONS

"Jacobean Tapestry" *by Pollack & Associates*
Madder
Viscose 61%, Cotton 39%

"Carriage Cord" *by Mulberry—Lee Jofa*
Moss
Cotton 100%

"Gleneagle Damask" *by Lee Jofa*
Loden
Acrylic 43%, Chenille 29%, Wool 28%

"Gainsborough Damask" *by Lee Jofa*
Sapphire
Cotton 85%, Viscose 15%

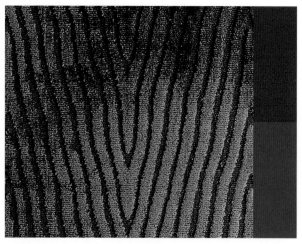

"Duquette Velvet" *by Groundworks—Lee Jofa*
Olive
Viscose 100%

"Joie de Vivre" *by Pollack & Associates*
Midnight Magic
Cotton 67%, Polyamide 22%, Polyester 11%

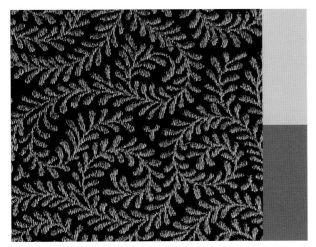

"Secret Garden" *by Pollack & Associates*
Tortoiseshell
Cotton 91%, Polyester 5%, Nylon 4%

"Muscat Grapes" *by Mulberry—Lee Jofa*
Claret
Silk 45%, Cotton 55%

"Basket Case" *by Donghia*
Blue
Cotton 50%, Mohair 50%

"Italian Damask" *by Decorators Walk*
Red
Silk 60%, Rayon 40%

"Villa Flori Damask" *by Decorators Walk*
Green
Rayon 53%, Cotton 47%

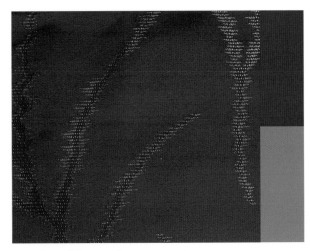

"Peachtree" *by Jim Thompson*
Flambeau
Silk 100%

LUXURIOUS FABRIC COMBINATIONS

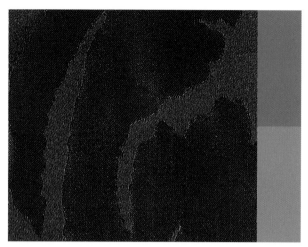

"Orleans" *by Nina Campbell—Osborne & Little*
Wine
Silk 100%

"Palmes Exotiques" *by Scalamandré*
Green/Madder
Cotton 100%

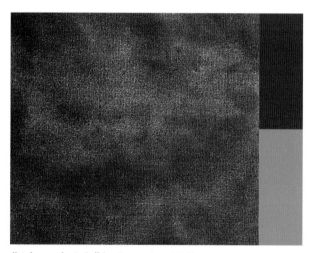

"Velours de Soie" *by Decorators Walk*
Coral Berry
Silk Pile 100%

"Davout Seme" *by Old World Weavers*
Green
Silk 100%

"Two Faces Have Eye" *by Gretchen Bellinger*
Butter Me Up
Silk 100%

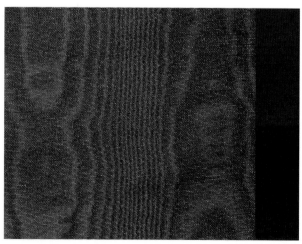

"Tempete" *by Creations Métaphores*
Caroubier
Acrylic 52%, Rayon 48%

"Regal Mohair" *by Home Couture*
Fig
Wool Mohair 100%

"Mapleton Cloth" *by Home Couture*
Vapor
Llama 51%, Wool 49%

"Ingenue" *by Maharam*
Peat
Linen 52%, Cotton 48%

"Angora Mohair" *by Groundworks—Lee Jofa*
Blue
Angora Mohair 100%

"Cashwool" *by Classic Cloth*
Hollyhock
Wool 90%, Cashmere 10%

"Landsdowne Chenille" *by Lee Jofa*
Cactus
Rayon 63%, Cotton 37%

Luxurious Fabric Combinations

"Panna Roma" *by Classic Cloth*
Borage
Mohair 100%

"Custom Aria" *by Maharam*
Pool
Cotton 100%

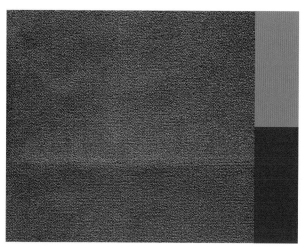

"Medoc" *by Old World Weavers*
Green
Cotton 100%

"Chippendale" *by Scalamandré*
Olive/Beige
Silk 75%, Cotton 25%

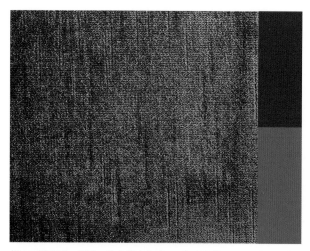

"Amalfi Velvet" *by G. P. & J. Baker—Lee Jofa*
Lichen
Viscose 50%, Cotton 47%, Modacrylic 3%

"Brocart de Lyon" *by Scalamandré*
Multicolor/Green
Silk 100%

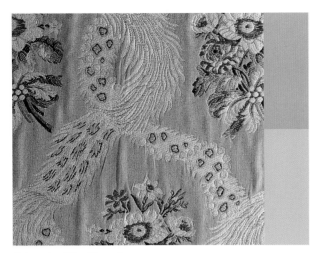

"Hermine" *by Pierre Frey*
Bourgeon
Viscose 85%, Cotton 15%

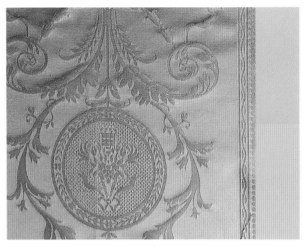

"Hepplewhite" *by Scalamandré*
Creme
Cotton 65%, Silk 35%

"Palazzo Pallavicini" *by Scalamandré*
Multi Sages/Paches on Cream
Silk 100%

"San Pietro Paisley" *by Lee Jofa*
Porcelain
Cotton 66%, Rayon 34%

"Serenity" *by Larsen*
Copper
Silk 67%, Wool 33%

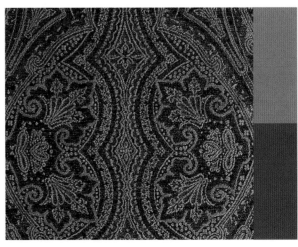

"Bitola Paisley Chenille" *by Lee Jofa*
Ochre
Cotton 75%, Wool 25%

ARTISTIC ELEGANCE

Intricate and royal

Elegant fabrics are the best in show and they have good reason to brag. Luminously colorful, richly adorned, and intricately woven or patterned, they are marked for their beauty, preciousness, and time-consuming construction. True works of art, embroidered tapestries and delicate crewel work require many hours of handwork or intricate machine processes for newer designs.

Chintz patterns, originally intended for royalty, are saturated with color, and so are usually glazed to enhance their bold patterns and to reflect light. Crisp, polished chintz in royal colors and rich patterns, used for king-sized bed coverings, pillows, and a ruffled canopy, engages the eye and makes weekend houseguests feel as if they are staying in a five-star hotel. A bright taffeta mimics a debutante's ball gown and adds life to a formal window treatment.

Whether adorning accent pieces or framed as works of art, these fabrics reveal the best in attention, design, and handicraft.

With their intricate designs and animated patterns, superior shine and luscious textures, elegant fabrics set a formal, engaging tone. Select them to lend a formal grace to a charming guest bedroom, a formal dining room, or a sophisticated library. These fabrics suit special places and special occasions.

OPPOSITE: Bright, glazed chintz drapes and pillows in intricate floral patterns mimic the gilded mirror and antique chandelier in this living room. Accent shades of green highlight the color of the exotic ferns beyond the window and provide a cool neutral to the playful floral patterns.

Decorating with Elegant Fabrics

Some elegant fabrics, including tapestries, thick brocades, and velvets, are thickly piled, full bodied, heavy textiles that require a delicate hand. Add a sturdy, high-quality linen backing to antique pieces or frame extra-fragile pieces as works of art. In smaller rooms, use them on a focal piece of furniture and add softer silk accent pillows for refined luxury. In large rooms with towering ceilings, display them as wall hangings, pillow coverings, or valences.

Lighter textiles, such as glazed cotton chintz, linen, and silk, add shine and color. They are versatile in smaller areas. Try them floor to ceiling, as curtains, pillow coverings, upholstery, or wall coverings. Go all out and deck a room in one favorite glazed chintz. Add accent pillows in a single complementary cotton solid and trim pillows and upholstery with plain piping or solid colored braiding.

BUILD THE LOOK

ELEGANT FABRICS SHOWCASE THE ULTIMATE IN EMBROIDERY DETAILS, ROYAL COLORS, HISTORICAL AND BOLD PATTERNS, AND THICK TEXTURES. THEY ARE RESERVED FOR THE ULTIMATE IN RICH, SOPHISTICATED ROOMS, FROM DINING ROOMS TO BEDROOMS TO SITTING ROOMS.

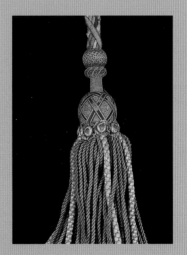

ABOVE: Bright, bold tassels like this one are an easy way to add elegant sparkle to pillows, curtains, and blankets.

OPPOSITE: An emphasis on details, from thick tassels to shimmery edging to hand beading, changes a look from ordinary to elegant.

Tips for Decorating
with Elegant Fabrics

✦ Chintz is pretty and popular, but by no means durable. It is best suited to small, delicate pieces, such as curtains, upholstery on elaborately carved dining or side chairs, and decorative table coverings. For a harmonious look in a small room, envelop the space completely in chintz: on sofa pillows, accent tables, draperies, and on walls as ultrafine wallpaper. Choose crisp colors such as green and yellow. Softly voluminous, this fabric also makes extraordinarily beautiful window treatments and curtains for an oversized canopy bed. Choose a favorite pattern in calming shades of blue and rose.

✦ Because of their delicate nature and time-consuming construction, embroidered works were reserved for very special places and very special people. Antique embroideries, in fact, can be quite costly these days and should be treated as works of art. Framed and hung on a wall, a priceless piece becomes the center of attention and a very special conversation piece. Machine embroidered fabrics can mimic the hand detailing of times gone by and look particularly pretty in small areas where their detail can be appreciated, such as on pillow coverings or tablecloths, napkins, and runners.

✦ Most elegant fabrics have heft and, thus, are somewhat limited in their use. Heavy tapestries work well as wall hangings, say above a headboard in a lavish bedroom, or as small accent pillows, but in general they are too expensive and heavy for upholstery. Thick velvet curtains require heavier and stronger support systems when used as window treatment. To counteract their heaviness, choose lighter colors (a glowing gold works well) to keep them from overwhelming.

ABOVE: Use glazed cotton chintz and silk to add shine and color. Versatile in small spaces, this gorgeous red and gold fabric makes the perfect throw for a reading chair.

OPPOSITE: Casual elegance is easy when you have the right accessories. A cleanly tailored sofa displays an array of smartly tailored pillows adorned with tiny jeweled buckles, fluffy tassels, and pretty embroidery.

Elegant color palette

Elegant colors touch the soul. They are warm, formal blues and intelligent, affluent reds put together to express a sophisticated charm.

Elegant Fabric Combinations

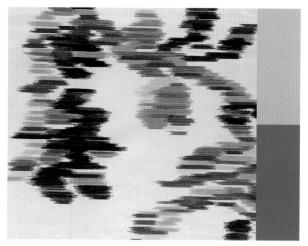

"Paradise Lost" *by Scalamandré*
Gold/Green/Multi
Cotton 100%

"Ashmore" *by Jim Thompson*
Gulf Stream
Cotton 70%, Silk 30%

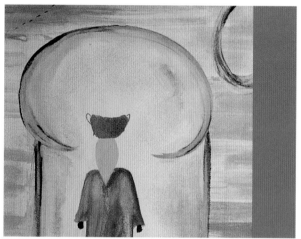

"Zanzibar" *by Pierre Frey*
Blue
Cotton 100%

"Ming Circus" *by Scalamandré*
Multi/Beige
Cotton 100%

"Collioure" *by Creations Métaphores*
Orme Armande
Acetate 100%

"Amanda's Peonies" *by Scalamandré*
Multi/Wheat
Cotton 100%

"Shangha" *by Scalamandré*
Multi/Cream
Cotton 100%

"Faucugny" *by Pierre Frey*
Blue
Cotton 92%, Viscose 8%

"Chinoise Exotique" *by Scalamandré*
Ecru
Cotton 100%

"Velours Louisiane" *by Old World Weavers*
Vert Moyen
Cotton 100%

"Laduree Velvet Stripe" *by Lee Jofa*
Rouge
Cotton 100%

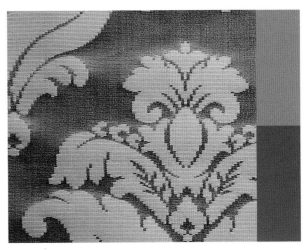

"Dogale Manin Damask" *by Old World Weavers*
Verde
Cotton 71%, Silk 29%

Elegant Fabric Combinations

"Le Gingerole" *by Scalamandré*
Lacquer Red
Linen 59%, Cotton 41%

"Renaissance" *by Classic Cloth*
Persimmon
Cotton 100%

"Porcupine" *by Lulu DK*
Green
Cotton 100%

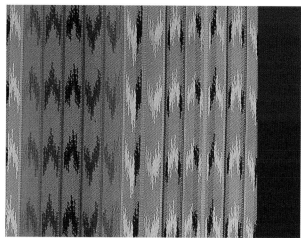

"Palissy" *by Pierre Frey*
Ecarlate
Cotton 59%, Viscose 41%

"Nonpareil" *by Pollack & Associates*
Willow
Cotton 53%, Viscose 47%

"Fayence" *by Pierre Frey*
Mordore
Cotton 100%

"River Qui" *by Scalamandré*
Multi/Taupe
Cotton 100%

"Zephyr" *by Creations Métaphores*
Laurier
Acrylic 52%, Rayon 48%

"Northwick Park Print" *by Lee Jofa*
Pale Lemon
Cotton 100%

"Cloisonné" *by Pollack & Associates*
Delft
Cotton 59%, Polyester 41%

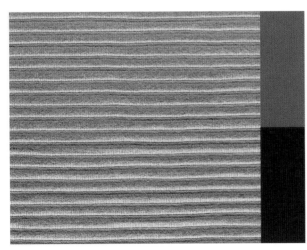

"Grand Otto" *by Classic Cloth*
Ginger
Cotton 70%, Rayon 30%

"Africa Toile" *by Scalamandré*
Blue/Cream
Linen 100%

Elegant Fabric Combinations

"Petit Palais" *by Scalamandré*
Classic Yellow/Greige
Cotton 100%

"Renaissance" *by Classic Cloth*
Sea Mist
Cotton 100%

"Cupido" *by Scalamandré*
Pink
Cotton 100%

"Applause" *by Gretchen Bellinger*
Tulip Time in Holland
Cotton 100%

"Strie Pin Stripe" *by Decorators Walk*
Chartreuse/White
Silk 100%

"Les Capucines" *by Pierre Frey*
Amande
Cotton 100%

"Tre Glazed Solid" *by Decorators Walk*
Green
Cotton 70%, Silk 30%

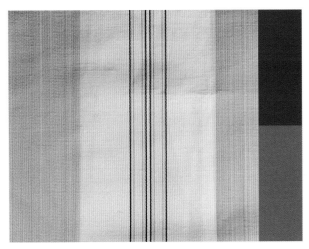

"Turandot Stripe" *by Scalamandré*
Green/Cream
Linen 63%, Silk 37%

"Rosebank Print" *by Lee Jofa*
Cameo Pink
Cotton 100%

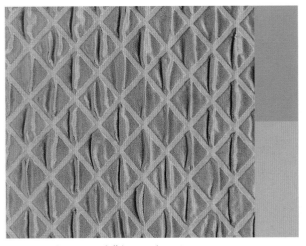

"Puckered Diamonds" *by J. Robert Scott*
Ice Blue
Silk 34%, Acetate 33%, Polyacrylic 33%

"Primavera" *by Scalamandré*
Cream
Cotton 75%, Linen 25%

"Clair de Lune" *by Scalamandré*
Pink/Aqua
Cotton 56%, Viscose 44%

FABRIC RESOURCES

Anna French

343 Kings Road

London SW3 5GS

United Kingdom

0171 351 1126

To the Trade Only

Brunschwig & Fils, Inc.

D&D Building

979 Third Avenue, Suite 1200

New York, NY 10022

212-838-7878

www.brunschwig.com

To the Trade Only

Classic Cloth

308 West Mill

Plainville, KS 67663

785-434-2777

To the Trade Only

Cowtan & Towt

20 Vandam Street

New York, NY 10013

212-627-7878

To the Trade Only

Creations Metaphores

485 Broadway

New York, NY 10013

212-725-2777

To the Trade Only

Decorators Walk

6851 Jericho Turnpike, #245

Syosset, NY 11791

516-861-3100

To the Trade Only

Del Greco Textiles

232 East 59th Street

New York, NY 10022

212-688-5310

Designers Guild

3 Olaf Street

London, W11 4BE

United Kingdom

0171 243 7300

www.designersguild.com

Donghia Furniture/Textiles Ltd.

485 Broadway

New York, NY 10013

212-925-2777

www.donghia.com

To the Trade Only

Gretchen Bellinger Inc.

P.O. Box 64

31 Ontario Street

Cohoes, NY 12047

518-235-2828

To the Trade Only

Home Couture

116 South Larchmont Boulevard

Los Angeles, CA 90004

323-936-1302

To the Trade Only

Interface Fabrics Group, Inc.

P.O. Box 179

9 Oak Street

Guilford, ME 04443

207-876-3331

www.interfacefabricsgroup.com

To the Trade Only

J. Robert Scott

500 North Oak Street

Inglewood, CA 90302

310-680-4373

www.jrobertscott.com

To the Trade Only

Jim Thompson Fabrics

1694 Chantilly Drive

Atlanta, GA 30324

800-262-0336

Knoll Textiles

105 Wooster Street

New York, NY 10012

800-445-5045

www.knoll.com

To the Trade Only

Laura Ashley

Freepost SY1225

P.O. Box 19

Newtown, Powys SY16 1LX

United Kingdom

0870 562 2116

www.lauraashley.com

Laura Ashley (USA)

7000 Regent Pkwy

Fort Mill, SC 29715

800-367-2000

Lee Jofa

D&D Building

979 Third Avenue, Suite 234

New York, NY 10022

212-688-0444

www.leejofa.com

To the Trade Only

Lulu DK Fabrics

136 East 64th Street, #2E

New York, NY 10021

212-223-4234

www.luludk.com

Maharam

251 Park Avenue South

15th Floor

New York, NY 10010

800-645-3943

www.maharam.com

Marimekko Oyi

Puusepankatu 4

Finland 00810 Helsinki

358 9 75871

www.marimekko.fi

Marimekko (USA)

1115 Weed Street

New Canaan, CT 06840

203-972-3685

Lucretia Moroni

Fatto A Mano Ltd.

127 Madison Avenue

New York, NY 10016

212-686-4848

email: lucet@ix.netcom.com

Oilcloth International

1959 Estes Road

Los Angeles, CA 90041

323-344-3967

www.oilcloth.com

Old World Weavers

979 Third Avenue, Suite 1002

New York, NY 10022

212-355-7186

www.old-world-weavers.com

To the Trade Only

Osborne & Little

49 Temperley Road

London, 8W12 4EY

United Kingdom

0208 772 2355

www.osborneandlittle.com

To the Trade Only

Osborne & Little (USA)

D & D Building

979 Third Avenue, Suite 520

New York, NY 10022

212-751-3333

Pierre Frey Inc.

12 East 33rd Street

New York, NY 10016

212-213-3099

To the Trade Only

Pollack

150 Varick Street

New York, NY 10013

212-627-7766

To the Trade Only

Rodolph, Inc.

P.O. Box 1249

Sonoma, CA 95476

707-935-0316

To the Trade Only

Rose Tarlow—Melrose House

8454 Melrose Place

Los Angeles, CA 90069

323-651-2202

www.rosetarlow.com

To the Trade Only

Scalamandré

942 Third Avenue

New York, NY 10022

212-980-3888, x515

www.scalamandre.com

To the Trade Only

Sina Pearson Textiles

150 Varick Street

New York, NY 10013

212-366-1146

www.sinapearson.com

To the Trade Only

Suzanne Tick Inc.

636 Broadway, Room #1200

New York, NY 10012

212-598-0611

To the Trade Only

Zimmer & Rohde

Zimmersmühlenweg 14-16

61440 Oberursel/Frankfurt

Germany

6171 632 02

www.zimmer-rohde.com

To the Trade Only

ACKNOWLEDGMENTS

I would like to thank Eva Michalek; the Sonet Agency; Jason Lowe; Andrea Loukin; and everyone at *Metropolitan Home*.

I would also like to thank Frank and Diane Bailey, the New York gang, Julie, and, most especially, Mudbug, Poboy, and Matt, for their patience and support.

PHOTO CREDITS